THE
RAG
DOLL
HANDBOOK

Ana Lakeland

B. T. Batsford Ltd, London

To Darin, Goran and Mitzy

First published 1991

ISBN 0 7134 6657 X

Typeset by Tradespools Ltd, Frome, Somerset

and printed in Hong Kong

for the Publishers
B. T. Batsford Ltd
4 Fitzhardinge Street
London W1H 0AH

Acknowledgements

The author and publishers wish to thank Sue Atkinson of
Arc Studios for all the photography, and Barry Newman and
the staff of Bekonscott Model Village, Beaconsfield and Mr
Cameron-Gudge and A. J. Sanderson & Sons for providing
locations for taking the photographs.

CONTENTS

$\mathcal{I}$NTRODUCTION

How these rag dolls came to life can be attributed, I suppose, to my overabundant sentimentality. As a child, I had always wanted to have my own cuddly doll to be a companion at play and my security at sleep, but the only one I ever received was a large vinyl doll in elegant attire that sat in a glass cabinet as a decoration not to be touched.

As the memories of this absence in my childhood continued gently to resurge years later, I began to attempt to handmake the rag doll I had always wanted: one that was lovely without being anonymous and adorable without being kitsch; one that a child could love and care for and make a part of his or her own life.

I attempted to sew numerous variations of a rag doll, taking bits and pieces from every source and ultimately combining what I learned with what I envisaged in my head. The result then, after years of experimentation, is the process which I share now with you in this book, and which I hope will produce the doll of your childhood as well ... or perhaps inspire you to create your own doll in your own way.

The custom of dollmaking has been around in various forms for a long time – in primitive rituals, in ancient ceremonies, as models for fashion designing and as playtoys for children.

It is only with the arrival of synthetic materials in the last fifty years that dollmaking passed from craftsmen to the industry and thereby became an anonymous manufacturing process. I hope, however, that this book will inspire you to try a more personalized and creative approach to dollmaking.

There are full-size patterns for creating each doll; each can be dressed and undressed, and the final doll should be about 35.5 cm (14 in) tall. In addition, a wide range of dressmaking techniques has been covered, which you can then utilize to design your very own creations.

$\mathcal{B}$EFORE YOU $\mathcal{B}$EGIN

TOOLS AND MATERIALS

Sewing machine

The sewing can be done both by machine and hand, depending on individual preference and ability. If you decide to use a machine, which would therefore speed up the process, you will need three basic stitches – straight, reverse and zigzag. Place your machine on a table in a well-lit room or near a bright lamp, as good lighting and comfort are essential for all sewing. Read your machine handbook if you are not confident with its operation, and practise on scraps of fabric before you make anything.

Needles

You will need to use size 11 for machine sewing, and I found in hand sewing that sharps (round-eyed, medium-length needles) suited all my needs. You will also need a long darning needle for working through very thick layers, such as embroidering facial features, forming a neck, and joining legs to the body.

Threads and yarn

For general sewing you should use threads that complement the fabric in colour and 'nature' (natural for natural and synthetic for synthetic). For embroidering facial features and a few other purposes, you will need three colours of strong thread (crochet cotton is ideal): white, pink and flesh-coloured.

To maintain a *natural* rag doll look, the choice of yarn for the hair is crucial. I tried to use shades that closely resembled natural hair and textures (like bouclé yarn) to achieve a wonderful natural fullness. Often I have resorted to embroidery thread as well, though it tends to be expensive.

Fabrics

I have used various tones of flesh-coloured *close-knit* jersey for basic dolls. Stockinette is an alternative, but you should use double thickness as the body can be over-stretched otherwise. Make sure that you work with the grain of fabric vertical – that is, when it can be stretched the most widthways. The fabric quantities, as well as suggestions for types of materials with which to dress your doll, have been given for each character, although ultimately the fabric choice is widely variable and should be determined by your preference. When choosing the fabrics for clothing, pay special attention to colours – it is important to find the balance between pastel, strong, subtle and bright colours.

I have used black vinyl for the doll's eyes (matt finish is best) and also for a few accessories on individual character dolls. The American Indian Squaw outfit is made from leather, requiring only small pieces that can easily be found in the local outdoor market or fabric shop, or perhaps from one of your old discarded leather garments or accessories. I have used a small swatch of felt only for the Clown's mouth, but don't use it as a replacement for vinyl and leather, as the quality is inferior.

Fastenings

For safety reasons and washability, I have used sew-on hook and loop tape for fastening most of the garments, but buttons, press fasteners, hooks and eyes, and thin ribbons can be used if you choose.

Stuffing

You should allow time for patient stuffing, as it is the secret to every rag doll. Use dust-free and fully washable, high-bulk, white polyester, and stuff only a little at a time carefully; pay particular attention to forming contours, as they will bring your rag doll to life.

Glue

All-purpose, clear adhesive is best for attaching the nose, eyes, hair and to prevent ribbon-ends from fraying.

Rouge

Use a pale shade of make-up rouge or blusher and apply it lightly to the doll's cheeks.

Useful tools

In addition to the standard sewing tools such as tape measure, pins, thimble, tailor's chalk, pencil, scissors, iron, you will find that the following are very useful:
● large screwdriver for turning pieces right-side out and for helping with stuffing the dolls
● large-tooth comb for combing yarn hair while glueing it to the head, and when making various hairstyles
● fine-tooth comb for more precise hair styling and also to unravel individual strands for fullness
● tweezers for handling small pieces such as eyes, noses, etc.
● leather- or paper-punch for cutting eye circles out of vinyl

Paper and card

You will need either cardboard or tracing paper for pattern making, and coverboard for box making.

HOW TO USE THE PATTERNS

The patterns are printed full-size, with the following two exceptions, which are too large to fit into these pages:
Rectangles (skirts, frills and bands) are made simply by using the measurements given within the appropriate instructions.
Half patterns are those rare pattern pieces that are too large to fit completely in this book. You can either cut them always on a fold in the fabric (the standard cutting method), or I recommend when actually making your own patterns that for these few 'half patterns' you place the dotted edge on a fold in the tracing paper or cardboard in order that, when unfolded, you have a complete pattern.

A 5 mm (¼ in) seam allowance has been included for all clothes patterns with the necessary exception of body patterns (where instructions explain the alternative procedure).

Use either of these two methods of tracing patterns:

1   Re-trace the pattern lines on the pages over carbon paper onto cardboard (this can be done using a dried-out pen in order to leave book pages unmarked). Then cut out the cardboard so that you have very durable patterns, which you can lay directly on the fabric and trace around with tailor's chalk.

2   Lay tracing paper over the patterns and copy. This is the more traditional method in which the light-weight patterns are then pinned onto the fabric.

It is important with both procedures to copy all notes within each pattern as well.

Each character has its own unique pattern instructions. However, a few items of clothing are used repeatedly, and in such cases you will be referred to previous pages for pattern illustrations.

Before arranging the patterns on the fabric you should determine if it has a design (perhaps a check or stripe) that might need matching for consistency. Also, line up arrows on the pattern with the grain of the fabric. You must then juggle the patterns until they all fit within the fabric piece. Now trace with chalk, or pin. Do not start cutting out before you have finished pinning all the pattern pieces to your material.

M E A S U R E M E N T S

I have included metric and imperial measurements throughout, although if you attempt to convert from one to the other you will find that they differ slightly – so it is probably advisable to use only one system.

S A F E T Y

This is just to remind you that very young children should not be given dolls containing buttons, pearl beads, or any small detachable pieces. With this in mind, the noses and eyes of these rag dolls have been attached both with glue and by stitching, making them childproof.

S E W I N G
T E C H N I Q U E S

Stitches

Machine
Running stitch
Longest stitch
Zigzag stitch

Hand
Backstitch
Gathering stitch
Overcasting stitch
Slipstitch
Cross-stitch

Finishing the fabric edges

Neaten all exposed raw edges on each fabric piece after making the garment, either by using a zigzag stitch on the machine or by overcasting the edge by hand. This will stop finished clothes fraying when they are worn or washed.

Pinning

When pinning fabric pieces together before sewing make sure that the pins are at right-angles to the sewing seams. This allows you to stitch directly over them and remove them afterwards.

Sewing the seams

Unless otherwise stated, all fabric pieces should be joined with the right sides facing. Only plain flat seams are necessary for stitching, and to secure their ends you should knot the thread at the start and finish when handsewing, or simply work some stitches in reverse if using a machine.

Hand stitches

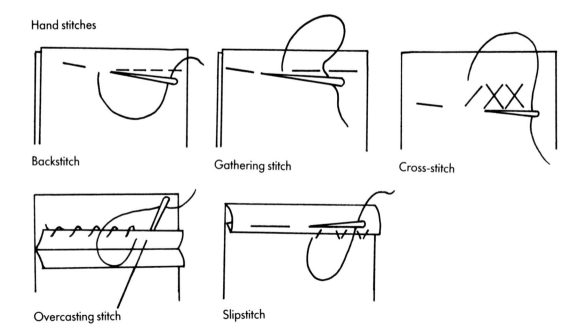

Backstitch

Gathering stitch

Cross-stitch

Overcasting stitch

Slipstitch

BASIC DOLL

M A T E R I A L S

Body and legs 28 × 76 cm (11 × 30 in) flesh-coloured jersey

Shoes 7 × 37 cm (2¾ × 14½ in) plain medium-weight fabric.

Optional: ankle-socks 30 cm (11¾ in) lace edging; knee-socks 10 × 20 cm (4 × 8 in) jersey

Hair 25 g (1 oz) thin yarn or embroidery thread

Stuffing 100 g (4 oz) white polyester

Eyes 1 × 2 cm (⅜ × ¾ in) black vinyl

Facial features 91 cm (36 in) strand of flesh-coloured crochet thread; 30 cm (11¾ in) strand of pink crochet thread; and 50 cm (19¾ in) strand of white crochet thread

I N S T R U C T I O N S

Doll's body

Trace the full Body pattern (page 15) on two layers of jersey, making sure that the grain of the fabric is vertical.

For long hair – mark the opening on top of the head and leave unstitched when sewing. Hair will be attached internally later on.

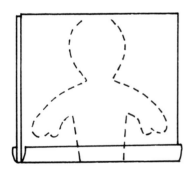

For short hair – simply stitch the top of the head closed. Hair will be applied externally later on. Also, with short hair there is the optional choice of adding ears. Use alternative pattern Body with ears (page 17) and sew 1 cm (⅜ in) into ears from top and bottom.

Turn up a 2 cm (¾ in) hem around lower edge and sew with a small stitch all around, following the traced marks. It is important to stretch the jersey slightly when sewing, so the seams do not snap when the doll is stuffed.

> I have not included the seam allowance on the Body pattern piece so that you can accurately stitch the doll form. It is therefore necessary that you form your own seam allowance by cutting carefully 1 cm (⅜ in) away from the seam line. Clip the curves.

Long hair

Wind the yarn or embroidery thread around the hair card. Cut the wrapped yarn or thread off the card with a single straight cut, lay it out flat, and then stitch at one end only, to keep the strands together.

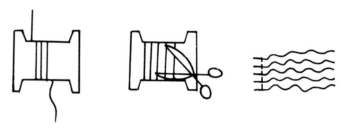

Insert the yarn into the doll from the bottom opening with the stitched side pointing towards the top of the head. Pull the yarn at least 1 cm (⅜ in) through the gap, sew over securely with a small stitch a few times to reinforce the seam and trim the excess yarn. As short hair is applied externally, it will be handled in a later step (see page 15).

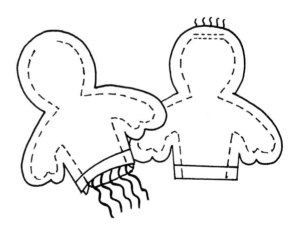

Legs

Cut two leg pieces, two upper shoe pieces and two of the sole pieces from their fabrics, and also ankle- or knee-socks if they are included in the character you are making.

Stitch together upper shoe pieces with the curved side of the leg pieces, matching them at points A and B. Insert a strip of lace for ankle-socks at the same time, or if making knee-socks, hem the top edges first by turning them under with stitching and then insert between leg and upper shoe pieces with wrong side of the socks facing right side of jersey. Stitch over the three layers of fabric following the curve.

Sew the sides of the legs together.

Take special care when sewing the sole pieces to the upper shoe pieces – do it slowly, easing one piece into the other following the curved edges, starting with point A on the sole at the open leg seam. Make sure that no unwanted pleats appear. Carefully trim the seam allowance to 2 mm ($\frac{1}{8}$ in).

Stuffing

Turn right sides of body and leg pieces out using a large screwdriver, being careful not to puncture the jersey.

First stuff the head and neck firmly using a little of the stuffing at a time to mould a firm and smooth surface. Then stuff the rest of the body and legs paying careful attention to the contours you are forming.

Don't stuff all the way to the brim of each opening, but leave 2 cm ($\frac{3}{4}$ in) unfilled.

If ears are included, take special care when bringing their shape out, pushing the screwdriver carefully into them all the way to the top and bottom to achieve a curled look. Do not stuff them at all.

Neck

First choose the smoother side of the head for the face. To form the neck, use a long darning needle and a single flesh-coloured crochet thread. Start the thread at the back of the head on the neckline and wrap it twice around the front. Pull it tightly to create a neck, and fasten off at the back of the head.

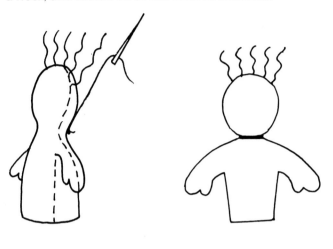

Joining the legs to the body

Push the tops of the legs into the opening on the lower body, making sure that the toes are pointing towards the front.

Use a long darning needle and single flesh-coloured thread and sew across the torso opening with a small stitch from one end to the other. It is important to stitch this point of the doll securely, as it is the weakest point on the body.

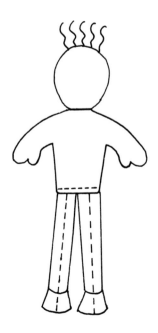

FACIAL FEATURES

Mouth

Start a doubled pink crochet thread at the back of the head, push the darning needle through to the front and embroider a 5 mm (¼ in) long mouth 2 cm (¾ in) up from the neckline in the centre of the face. Fasten off the thread at the back of the head.

Nose

Use 2 cm (¾ in) square of jersey, a fine needle, doubled ordinary sewing thread, and a small wad of stuffing to make a nose following the illustration.

Start a single flesh-coloured crochet thread at the back of the head and push the needle through to the face 1 cm (⅜ in) up from the mouth centre. Now pull the needle through the base of the nose matching its vertical grain with that of the face, and take the needle again through the head to the back. Now bring the same thread to the front again and make another stitch through the base of the nose in opposite direction of the first. Fasten off the thread at the back of the head. By making these two stitches cross one another, you fasten the nose securely. To reinforce it further, dab a little glue under the loose edges of the nose.

Eyes

Cut two eye circles out of vinyl with a leather- or paper-punch. Start a single white crochet thread at the back of the head and push the darning needle through to the face. Measure 1 cm (⅜ in) out from the sides of the nose and then 1 cm (⅜ in) up, and bring out the needle through this point.

Puncture an eye circle through the upper middle with the needle and return the thread through the face just above the eye. Fasten off at the back.

Repeat for the other eye.

Eyebrows

Using the same yarn as for the hair, thread the darning needle with a single strand. Start it at the back of the head, push the darning needle through to the face, and embroider lines in an angle suggesting eyebrows. Fasten off the yarn or thread at the back of the head.

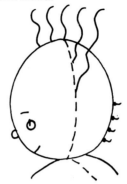

Cheeks

Using a pale shade of make-up rouge powder, apply a small quantity lightly to the doll's cheeks.

HAIRSTYLES

Long hair

Comb the doll's attached hair with a large-tooth comb spreading it evenly to cover the head.

Create a fringe at the forehead by shortening a few strands of hair to measure 6 cm (2⅜ in) from the centre top.

Lift the hair and spread the glue generously all over the scalp. Smooth the hair over carefully with the comb.

When the glue dries, use the fine-tooth comb to blend the individual strands together and add fullness.

Even the length of remaining hair.

Short hair

This hairstyle is used mostly for boys. To make it, wind a single strand of yarn or embroidery thread around one of your fingers 15 times or so, slip the loops off the finger and stitch them all over the doll's scalp securely.

Numerous other variations on the Basic Doll are given within the instructions for each character doll.

Leave open

BODY 'HALF PATTERN'

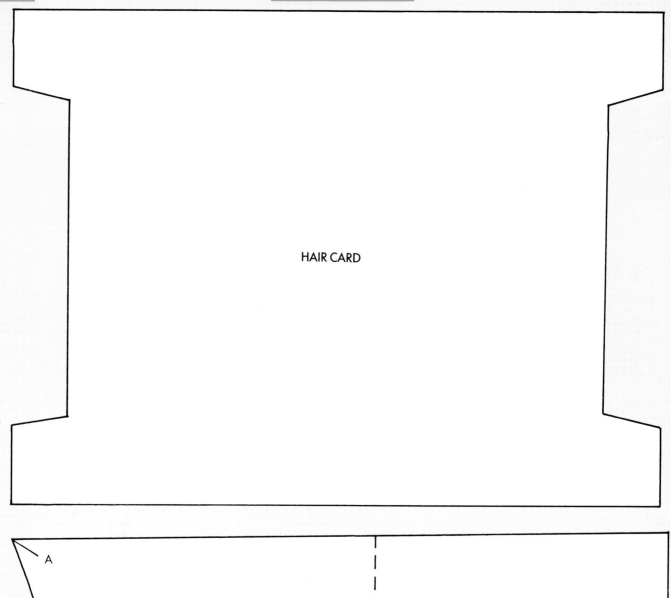

HAIR CARD

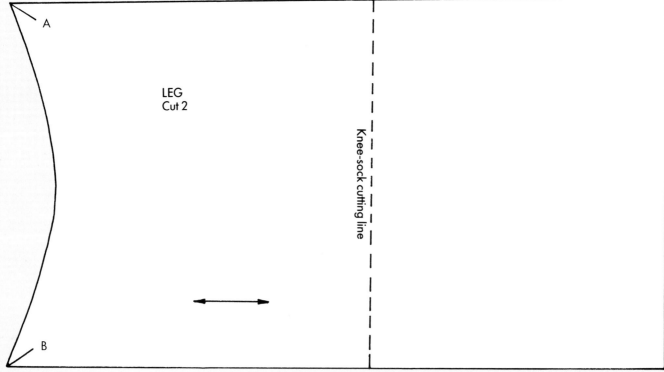

A

LEG
Cut 2

Knee-sock cutting line

B

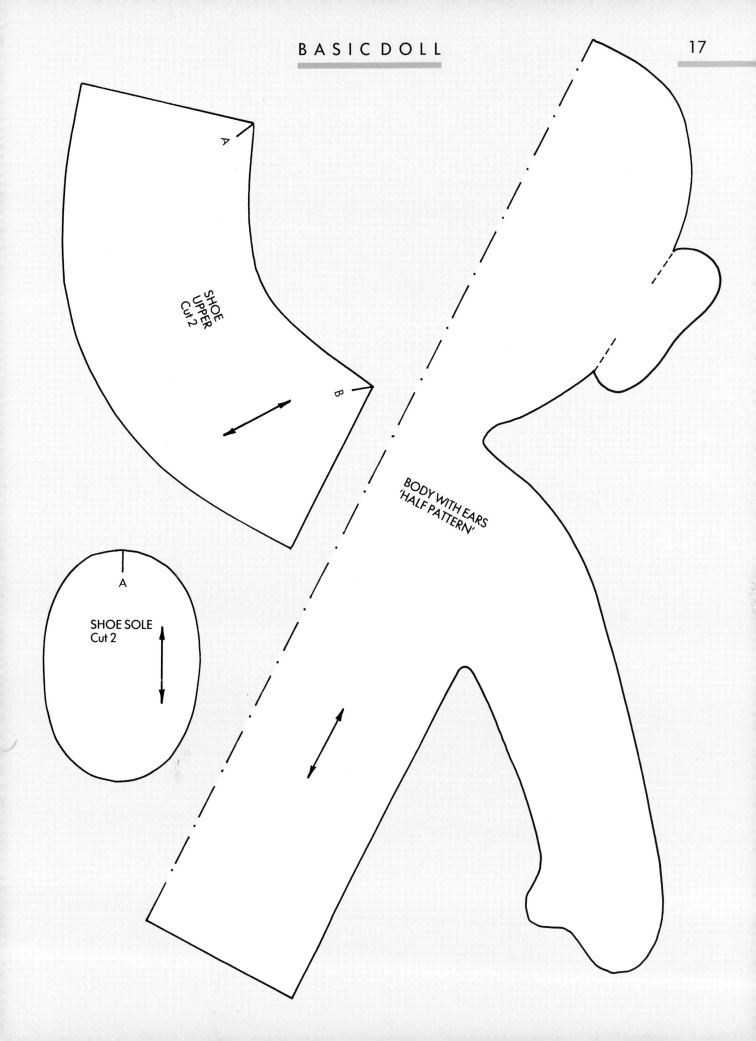

SHOE
UPPER
Cut 2

A

B

BODY WITH EARS
'HALF PATTERN'

A

SHOE SOLE
Cut 2

COUNTRY GIRL

MATERIALS

Hair bows 20 cm (8 in) narrow ribbon
Drawers and petticoat 20 × 95 cm (8 × 37³⁄₈ in) plain light-weight fabric; 40 cm (15³⁄₄ in) narrow elastic and 34 cm (13³⁄₈ in) narrow lace edging
Dress 20 × 100 cm (8 × 39¹⁄₂ in) patterned light-weight fabric; 62 cm (24³⁄₈ in) narrow lace edging; 7 × 26 cm (2³⁄₄ × 10¹⁄₄ in) plain light-weight fabric; 1 cm (³⁄₈ in) sew-on fastening tape and 20 cm (8 in) narrow elastic

INSTRUCTIONS

Doll's body

Make the Basic Doll with long hair and ankle-socks (page 12).

To make plaits, stitch the hair along the back and sides of the head just above the neckline and divide the hair in two equal parts at the nape. Plait the strands on each side and tie off the ends with the same thread or yarn as used for the hair. Trim ends to even lengths on each plait.

Make two ribbon bows by cutting the piece of ribbon in half and crossing the ends. Stitch around the middle with a thread of the same colour. Apply a thin layer of glue to the ends and trim when dry.

Stitch the bows to the end of each plait.

Drawers

Cut two drawer pieces out of plain fabric.

Turn under 5 mm (¹⁄₄ in) along the lower edges and cut a piece of lace edging in half. Place the two strips of lace edging to the underside of the hem on each drawer piece so that the scalloped edge falls just below the hemline. Stitch.

Now join the drawer pieces to each other by stitching along one crotch seam only. Open the joined piece flat and make a casing at the waist. Thread a 20 cm (8 in) piece of elastic through with a safety pin. Stretch the elastic to fit the doll's waist and secure.

Fold the drawers in half and stitch the other crotch seam closed. Stitch over twice at casing to reinforce the seam. Re-fold drawers into the finished form and stitch the inner leg seam closed.

Petticoat

Cut a 20 × 61 cm (8 × 24 in) rectangle from plain fabric.

Hem one long edge by turning it under with stitching and make a casing at the other long edge. Thread a 20 cm (8 in) piece of elastic through the casing with a safety pin. Stretch the elastic to fit the doll's waist and secure.

Fold the petticoat in half and stitch the side seam closed. Stitch over twice at casing to reinforce the seam.

Dress

Cut one front and two back skirt panels, one front and two back yokes and the sleeves out of patterned fabric, plus four collar pieces out of plain fabric.

To gather the skirt, sew two parallel lines of long stitches 1 cm (³⁄₈ in) apart between dots indicated on

the top edges of the skirt panels. Leave the loose ends of the thread at each end to hold, while pulling the fabric along the two threads, and spreading the gathers evenly.

Now pin the gathered top edges of the front skirt panel to the front yoke, and back skirt panels to respective back yokes (with armholes facing outwards). Stitch the seam through the middle of the two gathered rows, remove pins and then pull out the lower visible gathering thread.

Join the front yoke to the back yokes at the shoulders.

Make short full sleeves with frills by turning up a 2 cm (³/₄ in) deep hem at the sleeve ends and stitching a 10 cm (4 in) piece of elastic along with the hem. Stretch the elastic to fit as you sew.

Sew two lines of gathering stitches around the sleeve heads 1 cm (³/₈ in) apart and between dots indicated

on the pattern. Pull up the gathers evenly to fit the armholes. Lay out the garment flat and match side edge of bodice with sleeve underarm edge. Pin the sleeve heads to the armholes. To join sleeves to the rest of the dress, stitch the seam through the middle of the two gathered rows, remove the pins and then pull out the lower visible gathering thread.

Sew underarm seam and side seam of dress in one operation.

Turn under 5 mm (¹/₄ in) along the bottom edge of the dress and stitch it over, placing the raw edge of the lace to the underside of the hem as you sew. If both edges of the lace are scalloped, you can simply sew it directly over the finished fabric edge.

Hem the back opening edges by turning them under with stitching. The back opening is left unfastened except for a small strip of fastening tape that you attach near the neckline of both pieces.

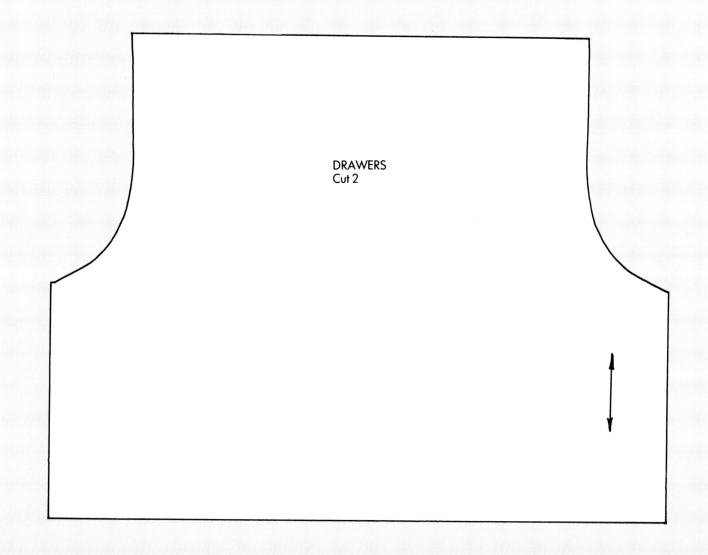

DRAWERS
Cut 2

To make the collar, stitch together the four pieces into two pairs along their outer edges. Trim the seam allowance carefully to 2 mm ($\frac{1}{8}$ in), turn right-side out, press and pin to the neckline on the right side of the dress, easing the curves one into the other. Stitch over, remove pins and then press the neck seam towards the dress and topstitch the hem under the collar to hold in place.

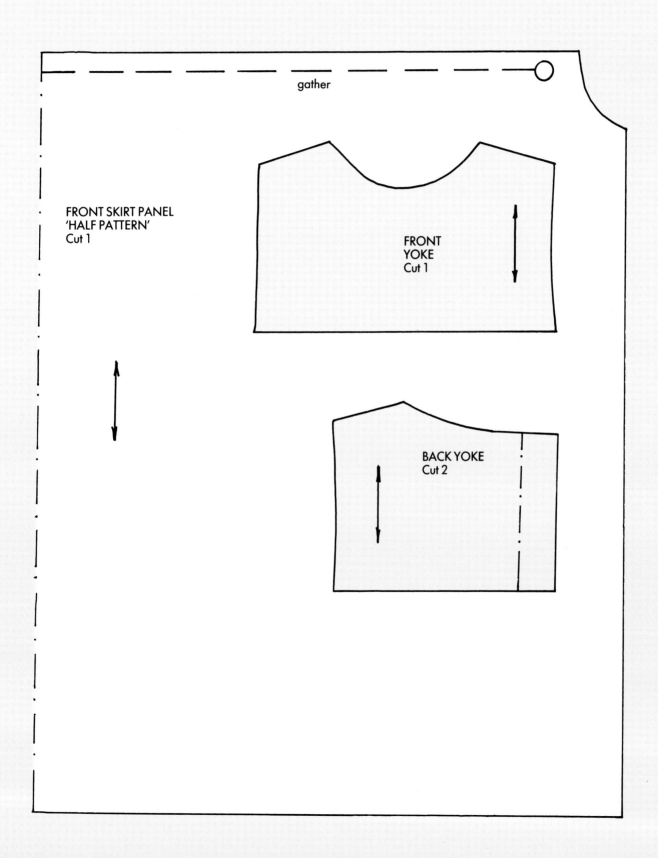

gather

FRONT SKIRT PANEL
'HALF PATTERN'
Cut 1

FRONT
YOKE
Cut 1

BACK YOKE
Cut 2

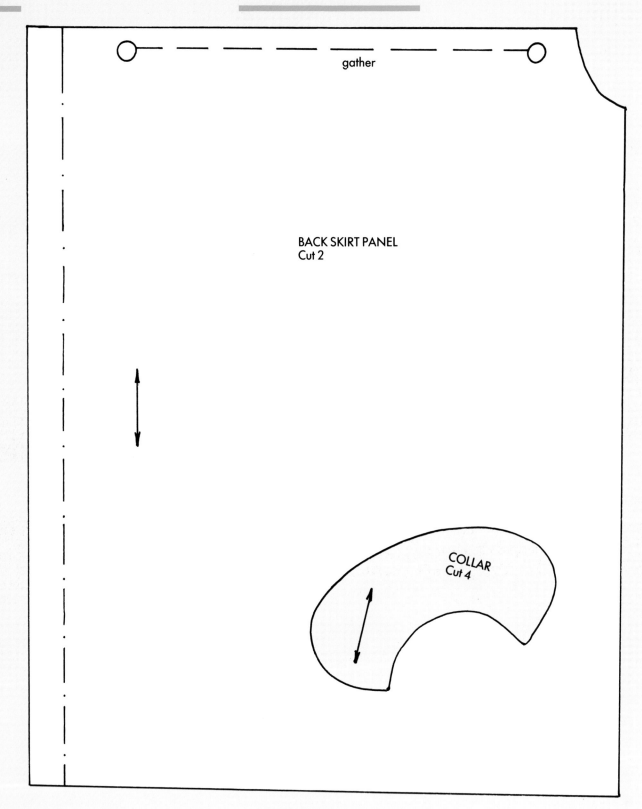

gather

BACK SKIRT PANEL
Cut 2

COLLAR
Cut 4

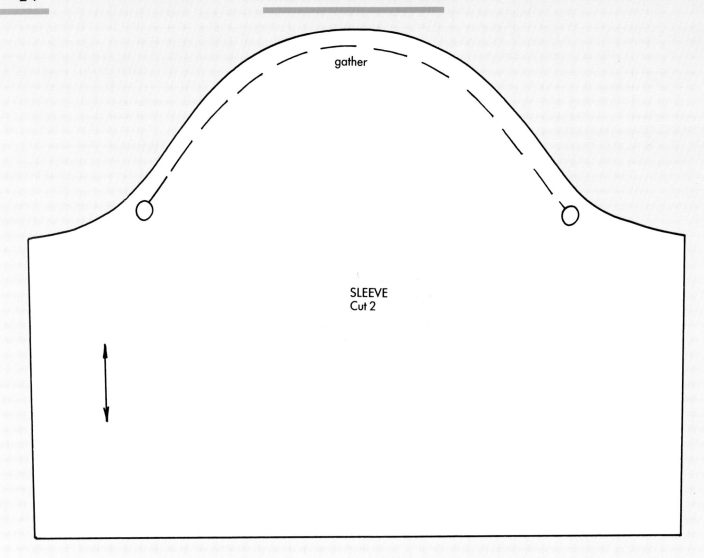

gather

SLEEVE
Cut 2

$\mathscr{V}$ICTORIAN $\mathscr{G}$IRL

M A T E R I A L S

Hair bows 20 cm (8 in) narrow ribbon
Pantalettes 17 × 34 cm (6¾ × 13⅜ in) plain light-weight fabric; 34 cm (13⅜ in) narrow lace edging and 40 cm (6¾ in) narrow elastic
Dress 10 × 150 cm (4 × 59 in) plain patterned light-weight fabric; 61 cm (24 in) wide dress trimming; 3 small pearl beads and 1 cm (⅜ in) sew-on fastening tape
Bonnet 15 × 52 cm (6 × 20½ in) plain or patterned light-weight fabric; 13 cm (5⅛ in) square of medium-weight iron-on interlining and 14 cm (5½ in) narrow elastic

I N S T R U C T I O N S

Doll's body

Make the Basic Doll (page 12) with long hair and no socks.

To make plaits, stitch the hair along the back and sides of the head just above the neckline and divide the hair in two equal parts at the nape. Plait the strands on each side and tie off the ends with the same thread or yarn as used for the hair. Trim ends to even lengths on each plait.

Make two ribbon bows by cutting the piece of ribbon in half and crossing the ends. Stitch around the middle with a thread of the same colour. Apply a thin layer of glue to the ends and trim them when dry.

Stitch a bow to the end of each plait.

Pantalettes

Cut two pantalette pieces out of plain fabric.

Turn under 5 mm (¼ in) along the lower edges, and place two 17 cm (6¾ in) strips of lace edging to the underside of the hem on each piece so that the scalloped edge falls just below the hemline. Stitch.

Stitch 10 cm (4 in) strips of narrow elastic to each pantalette piece 2 cm (¾ in) up from the lace edge to form a frill around the ankles. Stretch the elastic to fit as you sew.

Now join the pieces to each other by stitching along one crotch seam only. Open the joined piece flat and make a casing at the waist. Thread a 20 cm (8 in) piece of elastic through with a safety pin. Stretch the elastic to fit the doll's waist and secure.

Fold pantalettes in half and stitch the other crotch seam closed. Stitch twice at the casing to reinforce the seam. Re-fold the pantalettes into their finished form and stitch inner leg seam closed.

Dress

Cut one front and two back bodices, four sleeve pieces, a 10 × 61 cm (4 × 24 in) rectangle, and two collar pieces (page 22).

Sew the shoulder seams of the front bodice to the back bodice sections.

The Victorian Girl's sleeves consist of an oversleeve (upper) and straight sleeve (lower). First sew two parallel lines of long stitches 1 cm (⅜ in) apart along lower edges of the oversleeves. Leave the loose ends of thread at each end. Hold these ends while pulling the fabric along the two threads, and spreading the gathers evenly. Now pin the gathered edge of the oversleeve to fit the top edge of the straight sleeve. Stitch the seam through the middle of the two gathered rows, and then pull out the lower visible thread. Hem the lower edge of the straight sleeve by turning it under with stitching (unless you prefer to use an embroidered fabric, as I do, which does not need hemming).

Sew two lines of gathering stitches around the sleeve heads 1 cm ($^3/_8$ in) apart and between dots indicated on the pattern, and pull the gathers evenly to fit the armholes. Lay out the garment flat and match the side edge of the bodice with the sleeve underarm edge. Pin the sleeve heads to the armholes. To join the gathered crown to the bodice, stitch the seam through the middle of the two gathered rows, remove pins and then pull out the lower visible gathering thread.

Sew underarm seam and side seam of bodice in one operation.

To make the skirt, first stitch the trimming to the lower edge: turn under 5 mm ($^1/_4$ in) of the fabric and stitch, placing the raw edge of the lace to the underside of the hem as you sew. If both edges of the lace are scalloped, you can simply sew it directly over the finished fabric edge.

Now gather the waist edge of the skirt to fit the lower edge of bodice and pin. Stitch through the middle of the gathered rows, remove the pins and pull out the lower visible thread.

Join the edges of the skirt, taking a 1 cm ($^3/_8$ in) seam, beginning the stitch from the hemmed edge and up to within 4 cm (1$^1/_2$ in) of the waist edge. Spread the entire back seam and stitch along the V-opening to form a hem.

Sew strips of fastening tape (such as Velcro) at the top of the back opening for fastening the dress.

To make the lace collar, neaten the edges first and then pin the collar pieces to the neckline of the right side of the dress, easing the curves into each other. Stitch, remove pins and then press the neck seam towards the dress and topstitch the hem under the collar to hold in place.

Bonnet

Cut bonnet pieces out of their fabrics.

Place the interlining on one piece of the bonnet's brim and iron it on to the wrong side to stiffen it.

Stitch around the outer edge of a brim, trim the seam allowance carefully to 2 mm ($^1/_8$ in), turn right-side out and press.

Gather the curved edge of a crown to fit the inner edge of a brim.

Make a casing along the neck edge and thread the elastic through with a safety pin. Stretch the elastic and secure the ends with stitching.

Pin and stitch the gathered edge of a crown into the inner edge of a brim. Remove the pins.

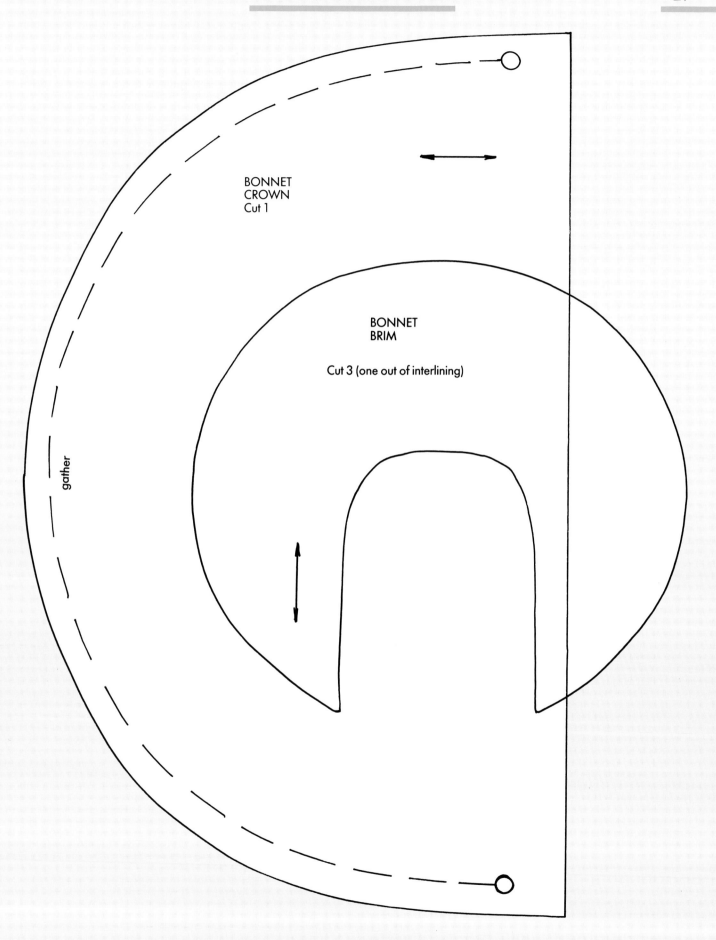

BONNET
CROWN
Cut 1

BONNET
BRIM

Cut 3 (one out of interlining)

gather

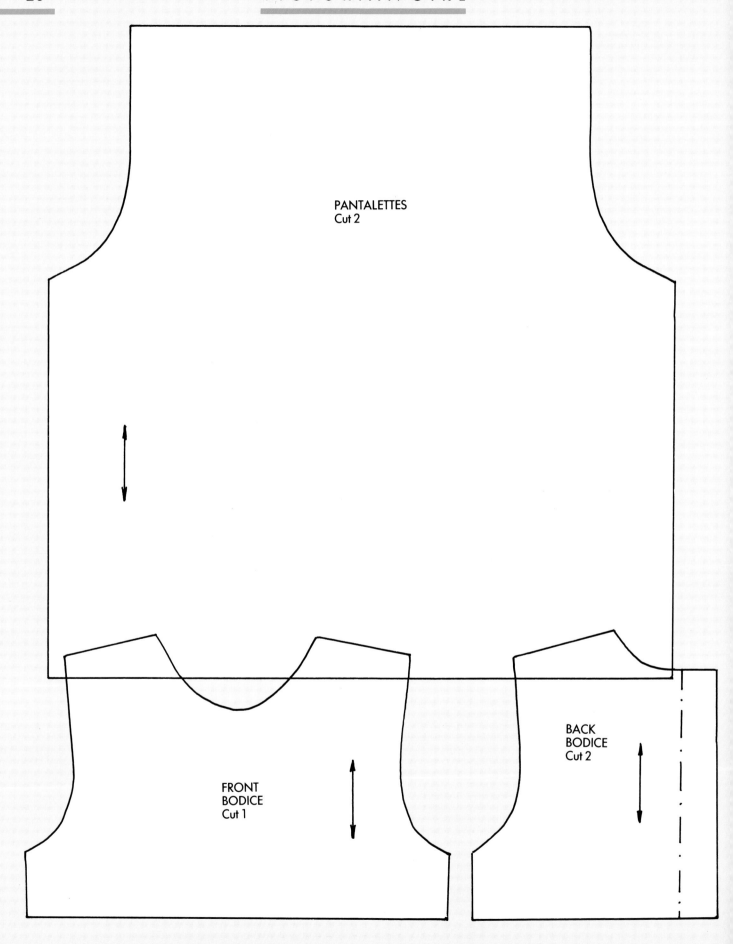

PANTALETTES
Cut 2

FRONT
BODICE
Cut 1

BACK
BODICE
Cut 2

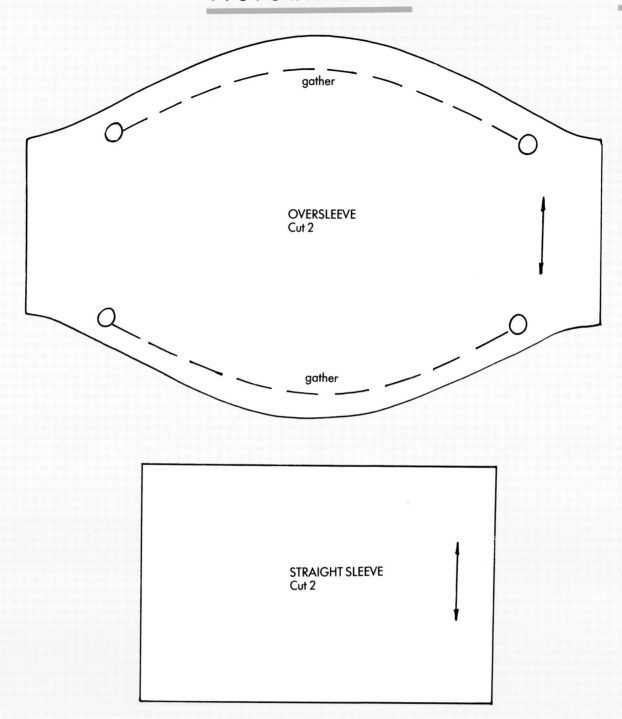

gather

OVERSLEEVE
Cut 2

gather

STRAIGHT SLEEVE
Cut 2

$\mathscr{V}$ICTORIAN $\mathscr{B}$OY

MATERIALS

Shoe buckles 2 cm (^{3}/$_4$ in) square of vinyl or felt
Shirt 15 × 65 cm (6 × 25^5/$_8$ in) plain light-weight fabric and 8 cm (3^1/$_4$ in) sew-on fastening tape 5 mm (^{1}/$_4$ in) width
Necktie 8 cm (3^1/$_4$ in) wide lace and 12 cm (4^3/$_4$ in) narrow elastic
Knickerbockers 17 × 37 cm (6^3/$_4$ × 14^5/$_8$ in) plain medium-weight fabric; 20 cm (8 in) narrow elastic and 1 cm (^{3}/$_8$ in) sew-on fastening tape
Cap 25 cm (10 in) square of plain medium-weight fabric

INSTRUCTIONS

Doll's body

Make the Basic Doll with ears (page 12) closing the top of the head to add short hair later, and including knee-socks.

Cut the shoe buckles from vinyl or felt and glue them to the front of the shoes.

Shirt

Cut one back bodice, two front bodices, sleeves, cuffs and collar pieces out of the plain fabric.

Sew the shoulder seams of the front bodice sections to the back bodice and turn under the front opening with stitching to form facings.

Slash and hem the sleeve openings and make pleats at the wrist ends as indicated on the pattern. To make cuffs, stitch the four pieces together into two pairs around the curved edges, carefully trim the seam allowance to 2 mm (^{1}/$_8$ in), turn right-side out and press.

To set the sleeves into the armholes, sew two lines of gathering stitches around sleeve heads 1 cm (^{3}/$_8$ in) apart, between dots indicated on the pattern, and pull the gathers to ease the sleeve crowns. Lay the garment out flat and match the side edge of the bodice with the sleeve underarm edge. Pin the sleeve heads to the armholes. Stitch, remove the pins, and pull out visible gathering thread.

Sew the underarm seam and side seam of the bodice in one operation.

Attach the cuffs to the wrist end of the sleeves from one slash to the other. Sew a 5 mm (^{1}/$_4$ in) piece of fastening tape to each cuff for closure.

Make a shirt collar by stitching the two pieces together around the outer edges, trim the seam allowance to 2 mm (^{1}/$_8$ in), turn right-side out and press. Stitch one side of the collar's neck edge to the outside neck edge of the shirt. Slipstitch the other side of the collar to the inside of the neckline. Top-stitch along the dotted line on the collar to form a foldline.

Hem the shirt by turning it under with stitching.

Sew remaining piece of fastening tape along the facings on the front of the shirt (the tape shown here is sewn with a zigzag stitch, adding a decorative look to the shirt's appearance).

Necktie

Cut the 8 cm (3^1/$_4$ in) piece of lace in half. Thin one of the pieces by 2 cm (^{3}/$_4$ in) and finish the side edges on both pieces.

Overlap the thinner piece on the thicker one, matching their straight edges, and stitch together.

Join the ends of the elastic, forming a loop, and stitch closed.

Fold the straight edge of the lace tie over the elastic band and hand sew the back (be sure the elastic join is concealed under the tie).

Knickerbockers

Cut out two knickerbocker pieces and two knee bands from the fabric.

Slash and hem the side openings on each leg piece. Now join pieces to each other by stitching along one crotch seam only. Open joined piece flat and make a casing at the waist. Thread 20 cm (8 in) piece of narrow elastic through with a safety pin. Stretch the elastic to fit doll's waist and secure. Fold the knickerbockers in half and stitch the other crotch seam closed. Stitch twice at casing to reinforce the seam.

Re-fold knickerbockers into their finished form and stitch inner leg seam closed.

Now gather the bottom of both pieces to fit the bands by sewing two parallel lines of long stitches between dots indicated on the pattern. Leave loose ends of thread at each end to hold, while pulling the fabric along the two threads and spreading the gathers evenly.

The procedure for attaching the knee bands is similar to applying bias tape. Fold the bands in half lengthwise and press. Lay the gathered end of the knickerbockers over one edge of the band, and pin leaving 1 cm ($^3/_8$ in) free on each side for overlappings. Stitch in place, remove pins and then pull out the lower visible gathering thread. Fold the band over, turning under the seam allowance, and slip-stitch it to underside of the leg, closing up the side of the band. Sew strips of fastening tape onto the overlappings.

Cap

Cut the crown of the cap, two brim pieces and the band out of fabric.

Fold the band in half lengthwise and join the side seam.

Pleat the outer edge of the crown (making equal pleats all around, tacking them in place) to fit the band loop.

Pin the crown to the loop and stitch over. Pull out the tacking threads.

Make the brim by stitching the two pieces together along their outer edges, trim the seam allowance carefully to 2 mm ($^1/_8$ in), turn right-side out and press.

Stitch the brim onto the band (making sure the side seam of the band is opposite the centre of the brim).

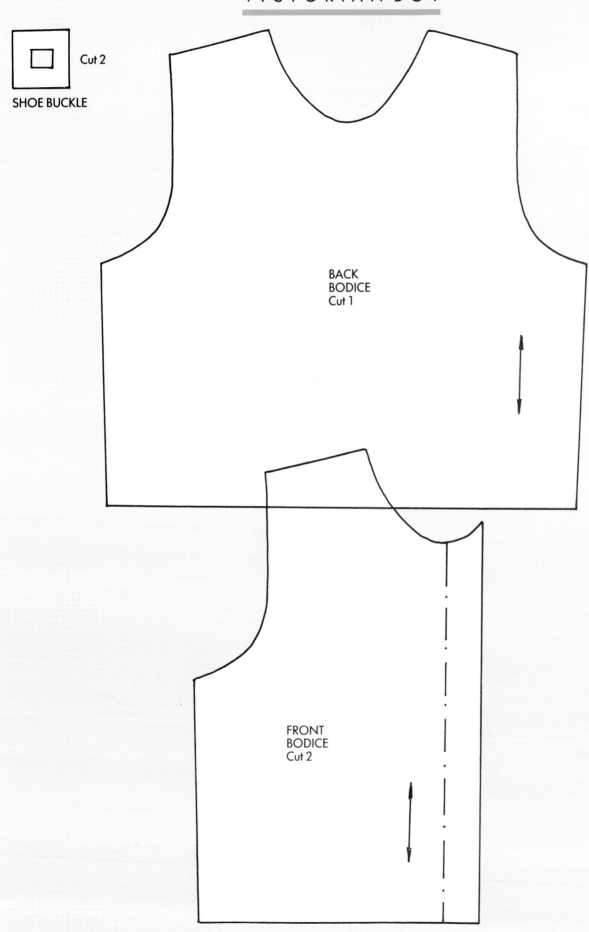

Cut 2

SHOE BUCKLE

BACK
BODICE
Cut 1

FRONT
BODICE
Cut 2

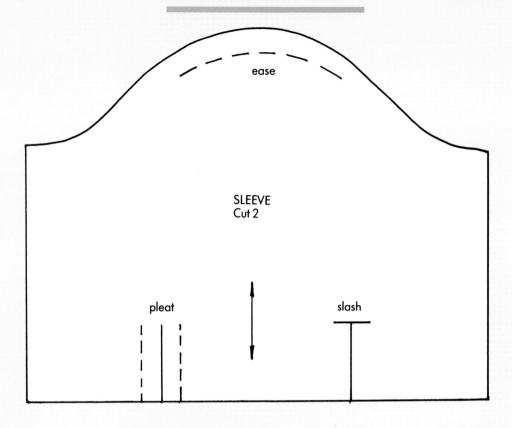

SLEEVE
Cut 2

pleat   slash

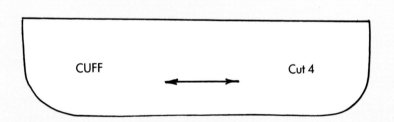

CUFF   Cut 4

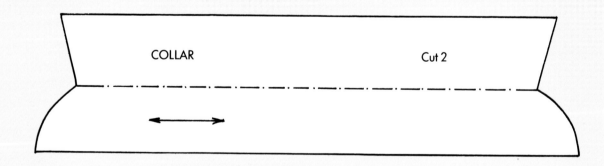

COLLAR   Cut 2

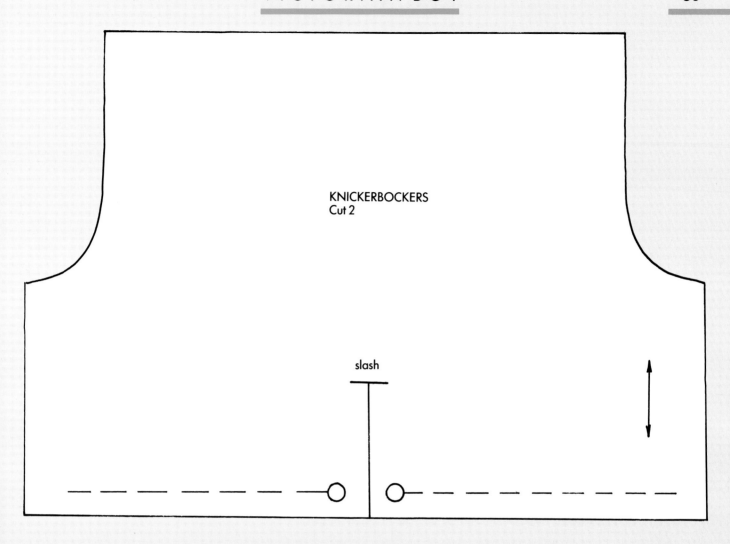

KNICKERBOCKERS
Cut 2

slash

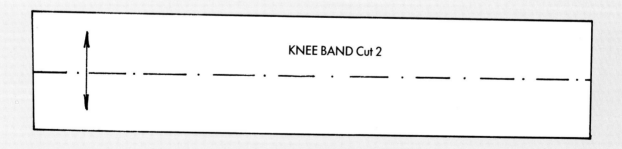

KNEE BAND Cut 2

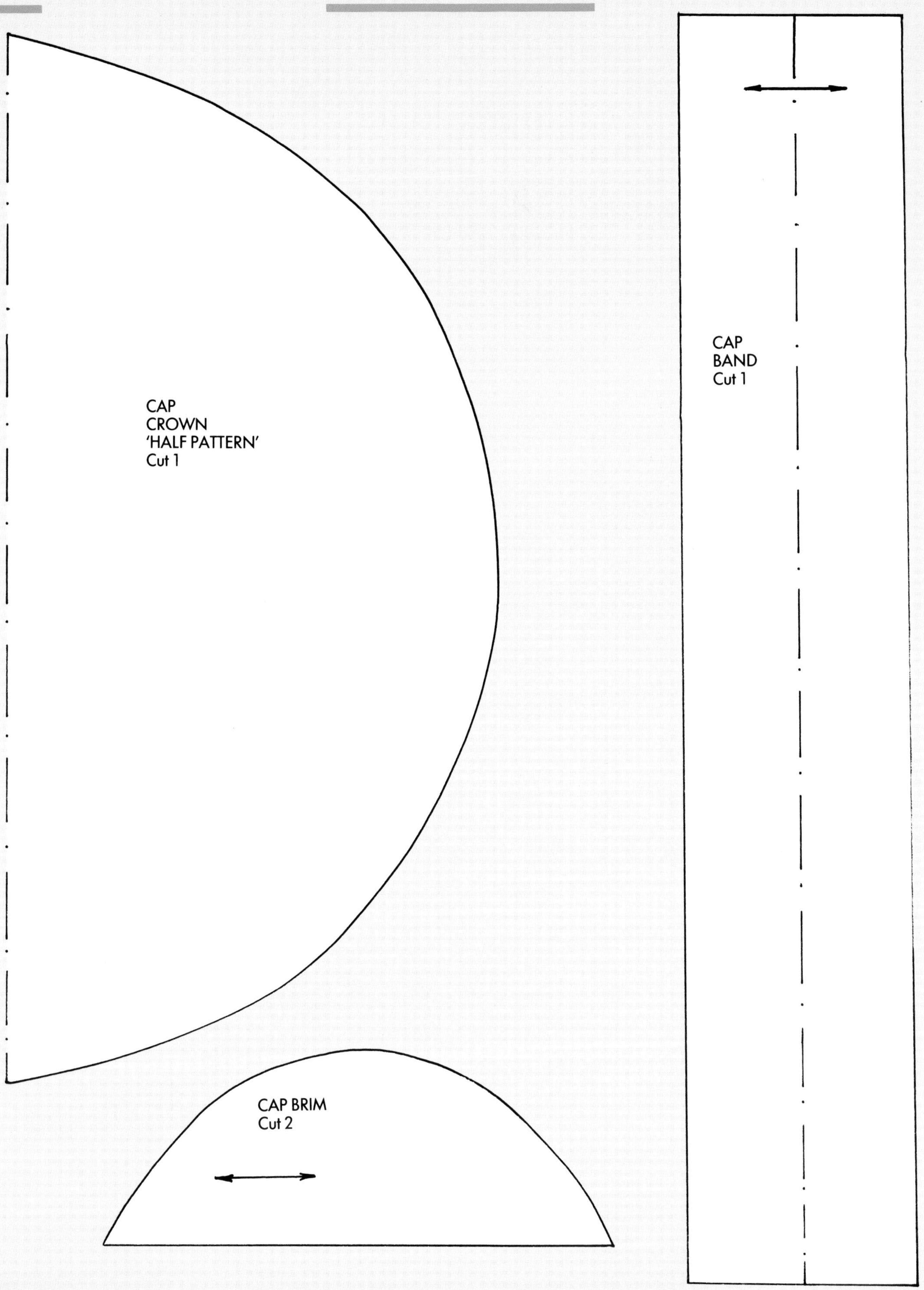

CAP
CROWN
'HALF PATTERN'
Cut 1

CAP
BAND
Cut 1

CAP BRIM
Cut 2

Sailor Girl or Sailor Boy

MATERIALS

Shoelaces 61 cm (24 in) strand of strong yarn or thread

Girl's underpants 9 × 30 cm (3$^{1}/_{2}$ × 11$^{3}/_{4}$ in) plain light-weight fabric and 30 cm (11$^{3}/_{4}$ in) narrow lace edging

Shirt 13 × 29 cm (5$^{1}/_{8}$ × 11$^{1}/_{2}$ in) blue and white striped fabric; 50 cm (19$^{3}/_{4}$ in) narrow blue or white bias binding tape and 1 cm ($^{3}/_{8}$ in) sew-on fastening tape

Girl's skirt/Boy's shorts, collar, sleeve bands and cap band 14 × 105 cm (5$^{1}/_{2}$ × 41$^{3}/_{8}$ in) blue light-weight fabric (girl); 14 × 78 cm (5$^{1}/_{2}$ × 30$^{3}/_{4}$ in) (boy)

Jacket and cap 16 × 87 cm (6$^{1}/_{4}$ × 34$^{1}/_{4}$ in) white light-weight fabric; 22 cm (8$^{3}/_{4}$ in) narrow blue bias binding tape; 25 cm (9$^{7}/_{8}$ in) wide blue ribbon (girl); 35 cm (13$^{3}/_{4}$ in) narrow blue ribbon (boy); 35 cm (13$^{3}/_{4}$ in) narrow blue ribbon; 40 cm (15$^{3}/_{4}$ in) narrow white ribbon; 2 small pearl beads (girl) and 8 cm (3$^{1}/_{8}$ in) sew-on fastening tape 5 mm ($^{1}/_{4}$ in) width

INSTRUCTIONS

Doll's body

Girl: make the Basic Doll (page 12) with long hair and knee-socks.
Boy: make the Basic Doll, closing the head gap to add short hair later, and including knee-socks.

Embroider a few cross-stitches with a single strand of yarn or thread on the front shoes for laces.

Underpants (Girl)

Cut two underpant pieces out of plain fabric.

Turn under 5 mm ($^{1}/_{4}$ in) along the lower edges on each piece, place strips of lace edging to the underside of the hem so that scalloped edge falls just below hemline and stitch.

Hem the waist edges and join pieces to each other by stitching along both crotch seams and then inner leg seams.

Shirt (Girl or Boy)

Cut one front and two back bodice pieces out of fabric. Sew the shoulder seams of the front bodice to the back bodice sections.

Hem the back opening by turning it under with stitching.

Cut two lengths of bias binding tape, each 17 cm (6$^{3}/_{4}$ in), and bind the armholes. Unfold one raw edge of the binding tape, and place it to the right side of the shirt with its edge level with armhole edge. Stitch along the crease of the binding. Fold the other pressed edge of the bias tape to the wrong side of the shirt and slipstitch along the hem.

Use remaining 16 cm (6$^{3}/_{8}$ in) of bias tape to bind the neckline in the same manner, with the exception that you will have to turn in the ends on each side before stitching tape closed.

Sew side seam of the shirt and hem the bottom edge by turning it under with stitching.

Attach strips of fastening tape at the top of the back opening for easy dressing.

Skirt (Girl)

Cut a 12 × 61 cm (4$^{3}/_{4}$ × 24 in) rectangle out of fabric.

Hem one long edge by turning it under with stitching.

Make pleats along the fabric piece choosing one of the variations given.

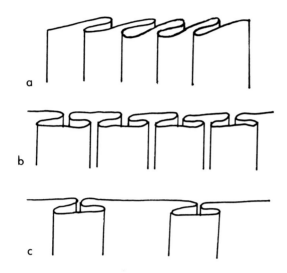

You can use the spacing and the size of the pleats for the effect that pleases you. Just make sure that the finished pleated skirt fits the doll's waist, that the pleats are identical in size, evenly spaced and that the opening edges are falling along the back fold of a pleat.

To attach the waist band along the waist edge, first fold the band in half lengthwise and press. Match one edge along the waist edge of the skirt and stitch. Fold the band back over, turning under a 5 mm (¹/₄ in) hem, and slipstitch it to the underside of the skirt, closing up the side ends of the band as you go along.

Sew on strips of fastening tape to overlappings for closure.

Shorts (Boy)

Cut two shorts pieces out of fabric.

Turn under 5 mm (¹/₄ in) along lower and upper edges on both pieces.

Join two pieces to each other by stitching along one crotch seam only. Open the joined piece flat and make a casing at the waist. Thread a 20 cm (8 in) piece of narrow elastic through with a safety pin. Stretch the elastic to fit the doll's waist and secure.

Fold the shorts in half, and stitch the other crotch seam closed. Stitch over twice at the casing to reinforce the seam. Re-fold shorts into their finished form and stitch inner leg seam closed.

Jacket (Girl or Boy)

Cut out two front bodices, one back bodice, sleeves, sleeve bands and two collar pieces (one for lining).

Join the front bodice sections to the back bodice at the shoulders.

Gather the lower edges of sleeves by sewing two parallel lines of long stitches 1 cm (³/₈ in) apart, between dots indicated on the pattern. Leave loose ends of thread at each end to hold, while pulling the fabric along the two threads, and spreading the gathers evenly to fit the width of the two bands.

Fold the band pieces in half lengthwise, pin over the gathering, and stitch. Remove the pins and pull out lower gathering thread.

To ease the sleeves into the armholes, gather the crowns in the same way as the sleeves, pulling the gathers to fit the armholes. Lay out the garment flat and match side edge of bodice with sleeve underarm edge. Pin the sleeve heads to the armholes and stitch the seam through the middle of the two gathered rows. Remove the pins and pull out the lower visible gathering thread.

Sew the underarm seam and the side seam of bodice in one operation.

Turn under the front openings with stitching to form facings, and sew strips of fastening (Velcro) along them for closure.

To make the sailor's collar, stitch together the outer edges of two pieces, carefully trim the seam allowance to 2 mm (¹/₈ in), turn right-side out and press. Attach the narrow white ribbon along the three straight edges, mitring at the corners, and stitching along both edges of the ribbon. Unfold one edge of the bias tape and match its edge to that of the curved portion of the collar. Stitch along the fold line, and press it completely to underside. Turn in ends of tape and slipstitch to the wrong side of the jacket. Hem jacket by turning under the lower edge with stitching.

Decorations

Tie a bow from a piece of the wide ribbon for the girl and sew it onto the right bodice just under the collar. Sew on the pearl beads for buttons.

For the boy, tie a piece of narrow blue ribbon under the collar.

Cap (Girl or Boy)

Cut two cap circles (one of them with a hole in the centre), and a band from the fabric.

Stitch the cap circles around the outer edges, carefully trim the seam allowance to 2 mm (⅛ in), turn right-side out and press.

Fold the band in half lengthwise, stitch the side seam closed and start pinning the inner edge of the cap circle along the band. When you have eased in the curve so it fits with no unwanted pleats appearing, stitch and remove pins.

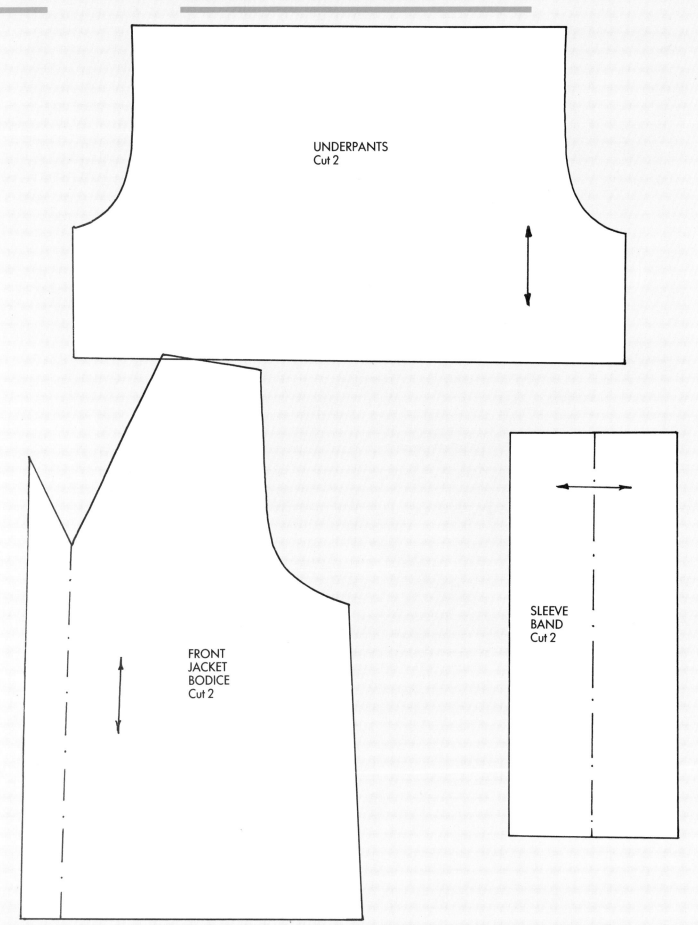

UNDERPANTS
Cut 2

FRONT
JACKET
BODICE
Cut 2

SLEEVE
BAND
Cut 2

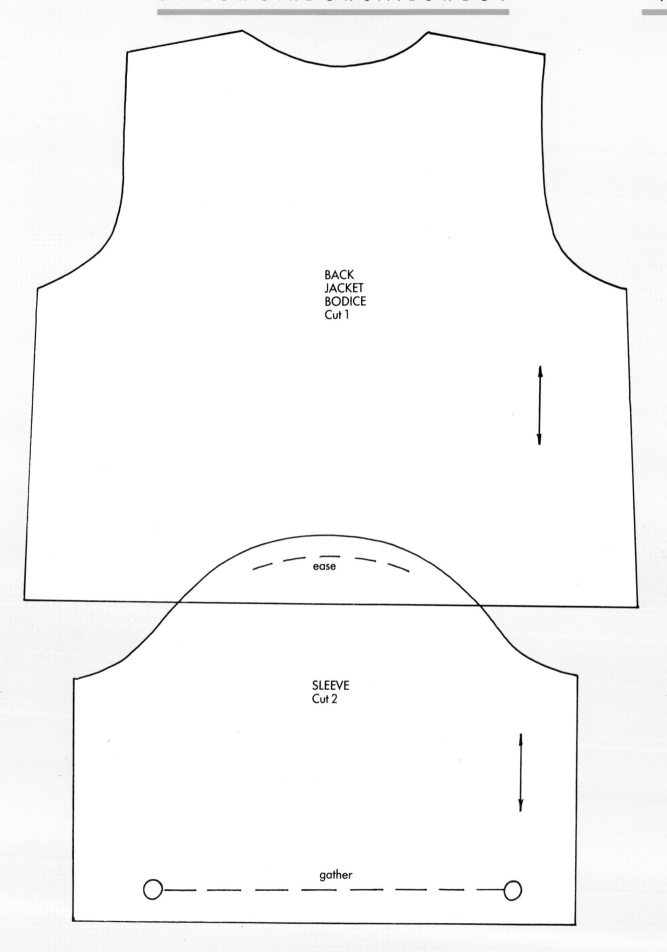

BACK
JACKET
BODICE
Cut 1

ease

SLEEVE
Cut 2

gather

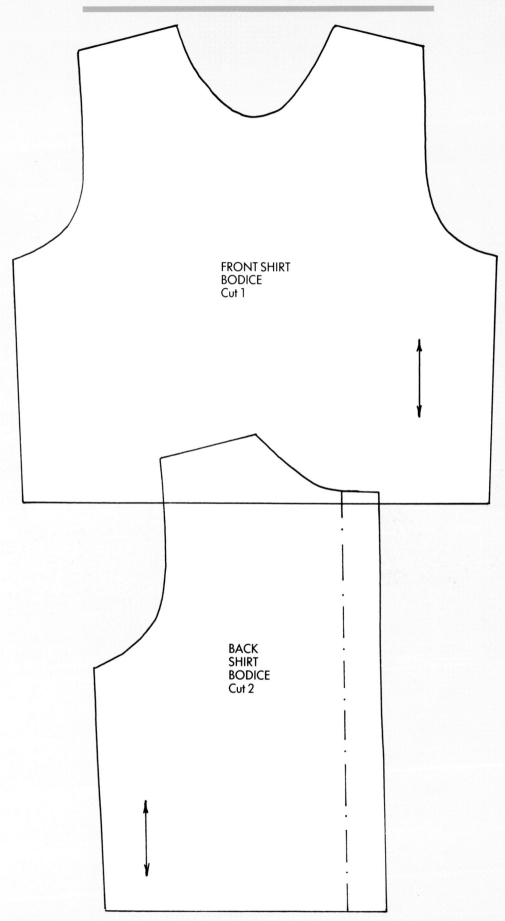

FRONT SHIRT
BODICE
Cut 1

BACK
SHIRT
BODICE
Cut 2

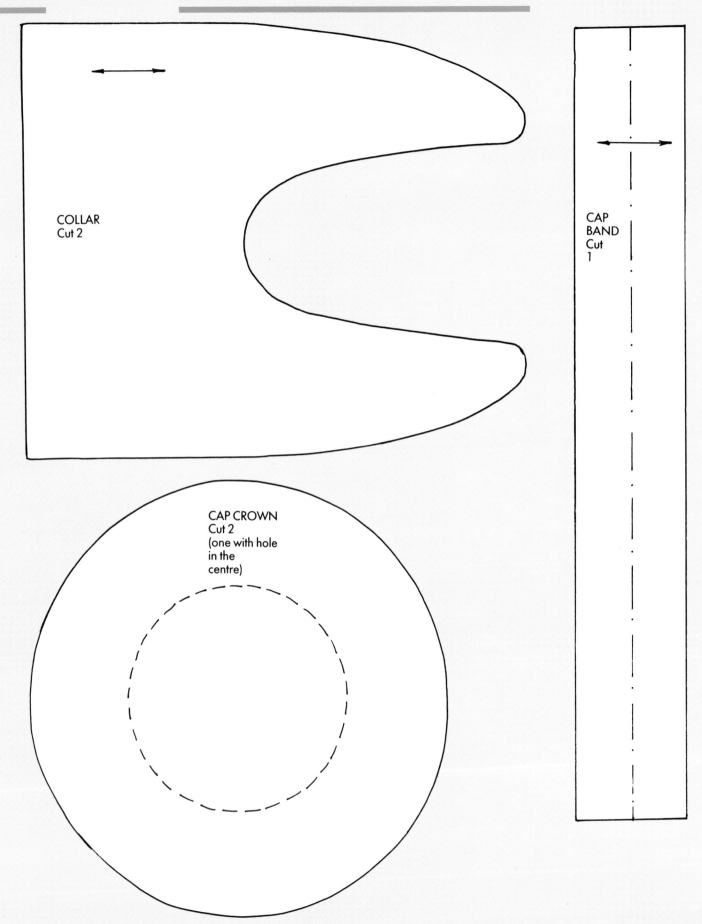

COLLAR
Cut 2

CAP
BAND
Cut
1

CAP CROWN
Cut 2
(one with hole
in the
centre)

$\mathcal{B}$ALLERINA

MATERIALS

Hair decoration 10 cm (4 in) decorative trim and satin flowers
Underpants 9 × 30 cm (3½ × 11¾ in) plain light-weight fabric and 30 cm (11¾ in) narrow lace edging
Bodice, flower petals and shoes 30 × 70 cm (11¾ × 27½ in) white satin and 20 cm (8 in) narrow ribbon
Skirt and shoulder frills 30 × 65 cm (11¾ × 25⅝ in) white netting fabric
Bows 30 cm (11¾ in) narrow ribbon

INSTRUCTIONS

Doll's Body

Make the Basic Doll with long hair (page 12) and use alternative pattern for legs and shoes as follows. Also, in order to create her hairstyle later, it is important that after cutting the fringe you do *not* glue the hair to the scalp.

Cut two leg pieces from jersey, and ballerina shoes from satin. Stitch together each shoe piece with a leg piece, fold in half and then sew up the sides of the legs. Turn legs right-side out and stuff firmly using a large screwdriver and a little stuffing at a time. Do not stuff all the way to the brim of each opening, but leave 2 cm (¾ in) unfilled.

Cut two pieces of ribbon, each 10 cm (4 in) long, and make bows, crossing the ends of ribbon and stitching around the middle with a thread of the same colour. Apply a thin layer of glue to the ends and trim them when dry. Stitch the bows to the front of each shoe.

To create the Ballerina's hairstyle, make a thin plait of a few hairs at the centre back of the head, roll it to the top of the head and hand stitch it in place. Now make two more plaits using some of the hair at each side of the head. Lift the hair and spread the glue generously all over scalp. Smooth the hair over carefully with the comb. When the glue dries, stitch the hair at the back forming a pony-tail. Hand stitch the decorative trim around the plait on top of the head.

Underpants

Cut two underpant pieces out of plain fabric using the pattern on page 40.

Turn under 5 mm (¼ in) along the lower edges on each piece, place strips of lace edging to the underside of the hem so that scalloped edge falls just below hemline and stitch.

Hem the waist edges and join pieces to each other by stitching along both crotch seams and then inner leg seams.

Dress

Cut three rectangles from netting, each measuring 10 × 61 cm (4 × 24 in). Also cut two front bodice pieces (one for lining), and four back bodice pieces (two for lining), 18 flower petals and two shoulder frills from their fabrics.

Join pair of front bodices along the neck edge and armhole edges. Trim the seam allowance carefully to 2 mm (⅛ in), turn right-side out and press.

Stitch pairs of back bodice sections along the neck edge and then along centre back. Trim seam allowance, turn right-side out and press.

Join the front bodice to the back bodice sections at the shoulders and along side seams.

Make flower petals by stitching the 18 pieces into nine pairs along their curved edges, leaving the straight edge unstitched for turning right-side out. Press the nine petals after turning, and pin them to the bodice along the waist edge leaving 1 cm (³⁄₈ in) free at either end. Stitch petals in place and remove the pins.

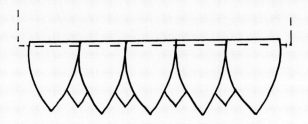

Gather upper edges of all three pieces of netting to fit the waist by sewing two parallel lines of long stitches 1 cm (³⁄₈ in) apart. Leave loose ends of thread at each end to hold, while pulling up the fabric along the two threads, and spreading the gathers evenly.

Now join the two edges of the skirt, beginning the stitch from the hemmed edge and up to within 4 cm (1¹⁄₂ in) of the waist edge. Spread the back seam on the skirt and stitch along the V-opening to form a hem.

Pin gathered upper edges of netting skirts to the waist and stitch the seam through the middle of the two gathered rows, remove the pins and pull out the lower visible gathering thread.

Cut a 20 cm (8 in) piece of ribbon in half and stitch two strips to the back opening for easy dressing and removal.

Make another bow (page 45) from the remaining piece of ribbon and stitch to the front bodice of the dress.

Gather shoulder frills between dots indicated on the pattern. Hand stitch them to the inside of the dress at the shoulders.

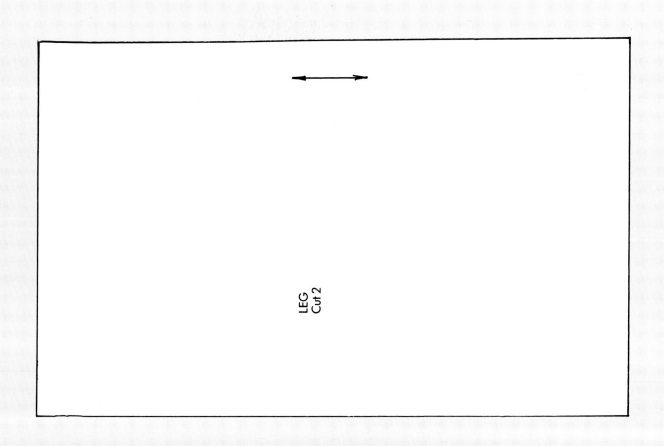

LEG
Cut 2

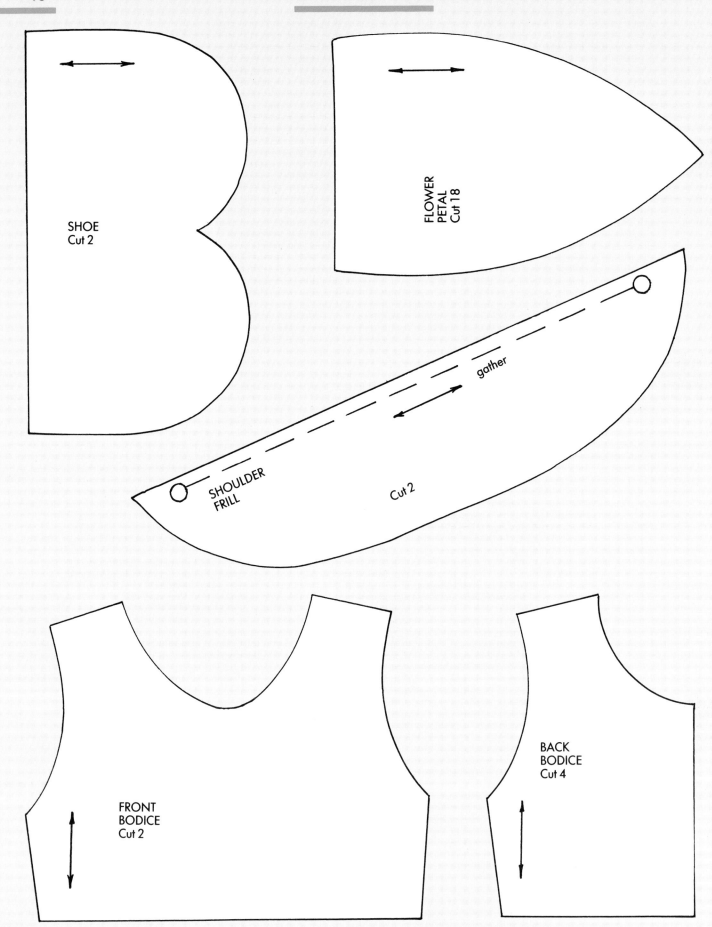

SHOE
Cut 2

FLOWER
PETAL
Cut 18

gather

SHOULDER
FRILL

Cut 2

FRONT
BODICE
Cut 2

BACK
BODICE
Cut 4

$\mathcal{C}$LOWN

MATERIALS

Body and legs 28 × 76 cm (11 × 30 in) flesh-coloured jersey

Shoes and bow 9 × 64 cm (3½ × 25¼ in) bright-coloured, light-weight fabric and 12 cm (4¾ in) narrow elastic

Hair oddment of bright-coloured yarn

Stuffing 100 g (4 oz) white polyester

Facial features 2 × 4 cm (¾ × 1½ in) white felt; 1 × 2 cm (⅜ × ¾ in) black vinyl; 4 cm (1½ in) square of red fabric; 91 cm (36 in) strand of flesh-coloured crochet thread; 30 cm (11¾ in) strand of red crochet thread and 50 cm (19¾ in) strand of white crochet thread

Shirt 13 × 56 cm (5⅛ × 22 in) checked light-weight fabric, 20 cm (8 in) narrow bias binding tape and 1 cm (⅜ in) sew-on fastening tape

Trousers 19 × 26 cm (7½ × 10¼ in) plain light-weight fabric (one half); 23 × 26 cm (9 × 10¼ in) plain light-weight fabric (other half and shoulder straps) plus two large 2 cm (¾ in) buttons

INSTRUCTIONS

Doll's body

Trace the full Body with ears pattern (page 17) onto two layers of jersey, making sure the grain of the fabric is vertical. Mark the gaps above each ear for hair, which will be applied internally later on.

Turn up 2 cm (¾ in) hem around lower edge and sew with a small stitch all around, following the traced marks and leaving the gaps above ears unstitched. It is important to stretch the jersey slightly when sewing, so the seams do not snap when the doll is stuffed. Also, make sure you sew 1 cm (⅜ in) into ears, from top and bottom, and close the top of the head. Clip the curves.

> The seam allowances have not been included on the Body with ears pattern piece so that you can accurately stitch the doll form. It is therefore necessary that you form your own seam allowance by cutting the fabric carefully 1 cm (⅜ in) away from the seam line.

Hair

Wind a bright-coloured strand of yarn 25 times or so around the hair card.

Cut the wrapped yarn along the two folds then, keeping the two bunches separate, stitch at one end of each to keep the strands together.

Now insert the hair bunches into each gap from inside the doll, and stitch over twice, reinforcing the seam.

Legs

Cut two leg pieces from jersey and two shoe pieces from bright-coloured fabric.

Stitch together shoe pieces with jersey at the ankles, and then, folding in half, stitch up the front.

Stuffing

Turn right sides of body and leg pieces out using a large screwdriver, being careful not to puncture the jersey. Take special care when bringing the shape of the ears out, pushing the screwdriver carefully into them to achieve a curled look.

Stuff firmly, using a little of the stuffing at a time. First stuff the head and neck, leaving the ears empty. Then stuff the rest of the body and legs paying careful attention to the contours you are forming.

Neck

First choose the smoother side of the head for the face. To form the neck, use a long darning needle and a single flesh-coloured crochet thread. Start the thread at the back of the head on the neckline and wrap it twice around the front. Pull it tightly to create a neck, and fasten off at the back of the head.

Joining the legs to the body

Push the tops of the legs into the opening on the lower body, making sure that the toes are pointing towards the front.

Use a long darning needle and single flesh-coloured thread and sew across the torso opening with a small stitch from one end to the other. It is important to stitch this point of the doll securely, as it is the weakest point on the body.

Facial features

Be sure to start and finish off all facial feature threads at the side of the head, just above the ears, so they can be concealed with the hair.

Mouth

To make the mouth, use the pattern and cut out of white felt.

Stitch it onto the face using a long darning needle and double strand of strong, red crochet thread, sewing two long stitches to form a smile.

Glue the edges of the felt to the face to reinforce it.

Nose

Using a 4 cm (1⅝ in) square of red fabric, a fine needle, red thread and a wad of stuffing, make a large nose as for the Basic Doll (page 14).

Using a cross-stitch coming through from a point above the ears, sew the nose to the face. To reinforce

further, dab a little glue under the loose edges of the nose.

Eyes

Using a leather- or paper-punch, cut two eyes from black vinyl.

Decide where to position the eyes on the face first, and then, centred under them, stitch a horizontal line that will extend 2 mm (⅛ in) beyond the black dot on each side.

Use a long darning needle and single white crochet thread. Bring the thread back through the face roughly 2 mm (⅛ in) up from the centre of the horizontal line, puncture the needle through the upper half of the black dot and carry the thread back into the face 5 mm (¼ in) above the centre of the eye (see illustration of finished Clown face).

Eyebrows

Embroider large eyebrows loosely using the same yarn as for hair and glue to the face in an upward curve.

To finish the Clown's body, unravel individual strands of yarn on the hair for fullness, even the length of each hair bunch and apply rouge to the cheeks.

Shirt

Using the patterns on page 42 cut one front and two back bodices, plus the sleeves (page 54) out of fabric.

Join the front bodice to the back sections at the shoulders.

Hem the lower edges of the sleeves by turning them under with stitching. To set them into the armholes, lay the garment out flat and match the side edge of the bodice with the sleeve underarm edge. Pin the sleeve heads to the armholes and stitch. Remove pins.

Sew the underarm seam and the side seam of bodice in one operation. Turn under back opening with stitching and attach strips of fastening tape to back bodices for closure.

To bind the neck edge unfold one raw edge of the binding tape, place it to the right side of the shirt (with bias tape edge level with the neck edge), and stitch along the crease of the binding. Fold the other pressed edge of bias tape to the wrong side of the shirt, turn in the ends on each side and slipstitch along the hem.

Hem the shirt by turning under the bottom edge with stitching.

Bow

Cut out bow pieces and bow knot from fabric.

Stitch together two bow pieces leaving an opening through which to turn right-side out. Slipstitch the opening closed.

Fold bow knot piece in half lengthwise and stitch along the length. Trim the seam allowance to 2 mm (1/8 in), turn right-side out and press. Topstitch close to both edges if desired.

Pleat the bow by hand nicely, then wrap the bow knot around and stitch it closed. Stitch the bow to the piece of elastic and pull over the Clown's head.

Trousers

Cut two trouser pieces and two shoulder straps from their fabrics.

Hem the top and bottom of each trouser piece. Sew along both crotch seams and then the inner leg seam.

To make shoulder straps, fold each strip of fabric in half lengthwise and stitch along the length. Trim the seam allowance to 2 mm (1/8 in), turn right-side out and press. Topstitch close to both edges if desired.

Stitch finished shoulder straps to inside of back waist, cross them over and stitch them to the underside of the front. Sew on the buttons.

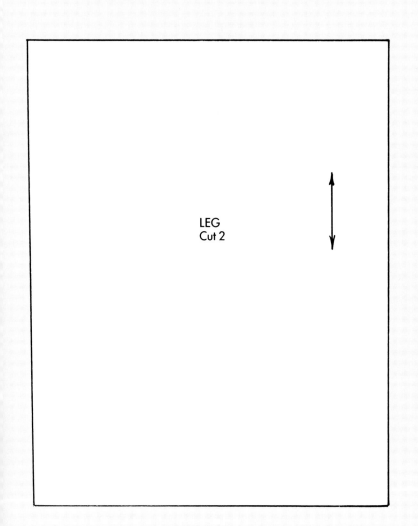

LEG
Cut 2

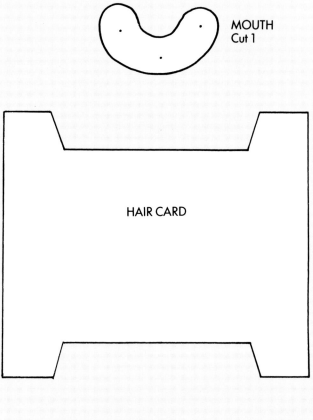

MOUTH
Cut 1

HAIR CARD

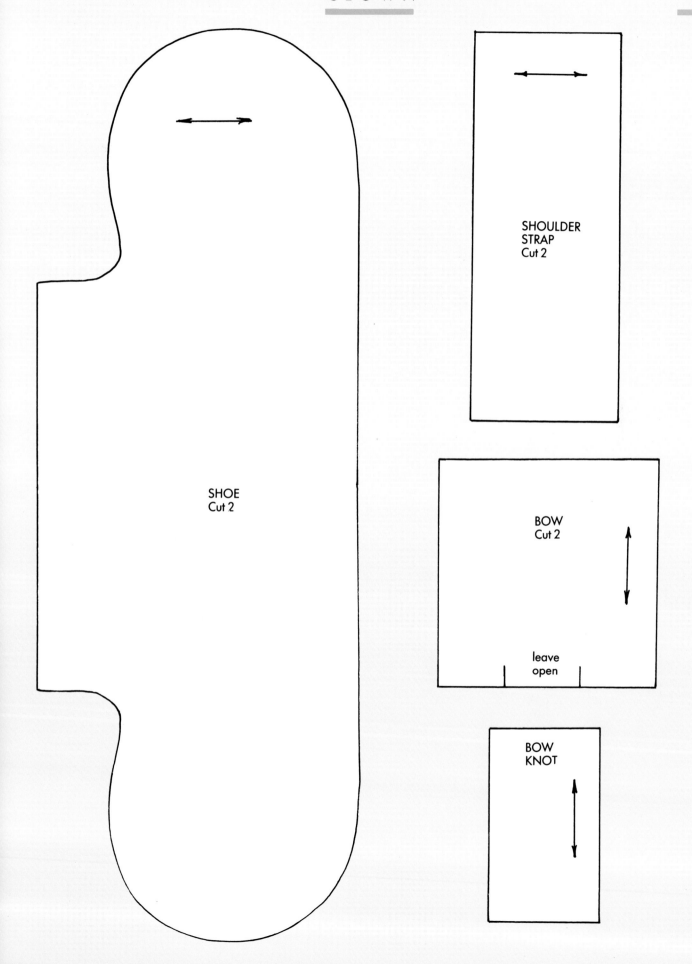

SHOULDER
STRAP
Cut 2

SHOE
Cut 2

BOW
Cut 2

leave
open

BOW
KNOT

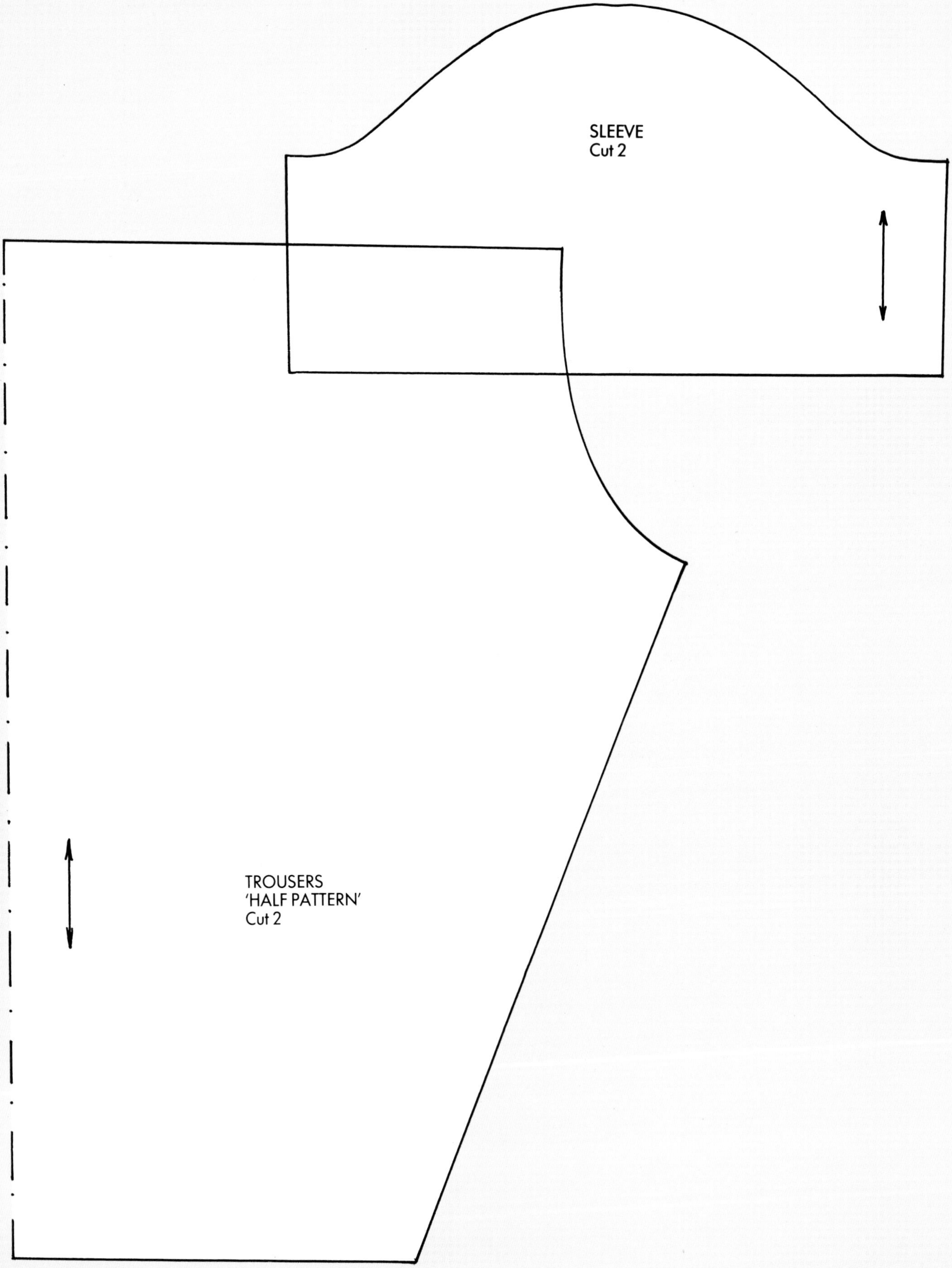

SLEEVE
Cut 2

TROUSERS
'HALF PATTERN'
Cut 2

$\mathscr{P}$IRATE $\mathscr{B}$OY

MATERIALS

Shoe buckles 2 cm ($^3/_4$ in) square of vinyl or felt
Earring small curtain ring
Eye patch 1 cm ($^3/_8$ in) square of black vinyl
Headscarf 15 × 25 cm ($5^7/_8$ × $9^7/_8$ in) spotted light-weight fabric
Shirt 15 × 80 cm ($5^7/_8$ × $31^1/_2$ in) plain light-weight fabric; 25 cm ($9^7/_8$ in) strong thread and 1 cm ($^3/_8$ in) sew-on fastening tape
Trousers and sash 22 × 44 cm ($8^5/_8$ × $17^3/_8$ in) plain light-weight fabric and 20 cm (8 in) narrow elastic
Sword 7 × 10 cm ($2^3/_4$ × 4 in) leather or vinyl

INSTRUCTIONS

Doll's body

Make the Basic Doll with long hair and no socks (page 12).

Trim the hair short so it reaches the base of the neck.

Embroider a moustache with the same thread or yarn as used for the hair.

Hand stitch the curtain ring to make an earring on either side of the head.

Cut shoe buckles (page 33) and glue them to the front of the shoes.

Eye patch

Cut one eye patch from vinyl.

Thread a needle with a doubled black thread and start it at the back of the head. Bring the thread across the face towards the eye and puncture through the edge of the eye patch from the right side. Now puncture the other edge from the wrong side and glue the patch to the eye. Finish off the thread at the back of the head.

Headscarf

Cut one headscarf piece from fabric.

Hem all three edges by turning them under with stitching and tie the scarf round the head, knotting the ends at the back.

Shirt

Using the patterns on pages 33–4 cut one back bodice, two front bodices and cuffs plus collar and sleeve pieces (pages 56–7).

Sew the shoulder seams of the front bodice sections to the back bodice and turn under the seam allowance along front opening. Stitch, beginning from the bottom edge and up to 5 cm (2 in) of the neck edge. Spread the entire seam and press.

Now slash and hem the sleeve openings and gather the wrist edges by using two parallel lines of long stitches 1 cm ($^3/_8$ in) apart. Pull the gathers to ease the fullness of the wrist edge into the cuffs.

To make cuffs, stitch the four pieces together into two pairs around the curved edges, carefully trim the seam allowance to 2 mm ($^1/_8$ in), turn right-side out and press.

To set the sleeves into the armholes, sew two lines of gathering stitches around sleeve heads 1 cm ($^3/_8$ in) apart, between dots indicated on the pattern, and pull the gathers, spreading them evenly. Lay the garment out flat and match the side edge of the bodice with the sleeve underarm edge. Pin the sleeve heads to the armholes. Stitch over, remove the pins, and pull out lower visible gathering thread.

Sew the underarm seam and the side seam of bodice in one operation.

Now attach the cuffs to the wrist ends of the sleeves from one slash to the other. Cut 1 cm (³/₈ in) piece of fastening tape in half and sew to each cuff for closure.

Make a shirt collar by stitching the two pieces together around the outer edge, trim the seam allowance to 2 mm (¹/₈ in), turn right-side out and press. Pin the neck edge of the collar to the neck edge of the shirt and stitch over. Remove the pins.

Hem the shirt by turning it under with stitching. Embroider a few cross-stitches up the front opening with a single strand of strong black thread, leaving a bit at the ends dangling.

Trousers

Cut two trouser pieces and one sash piece from fabric.

Hem the bottom edges on each trouser piece, and then stitch the two pieces together along one crotch seam only.

Open joined piece flat and make a casing at the waist. Thread a piece of elastic through with a safety pin. Stretch the elastic to fit the doll's waist and secure.

Fold the trousers in half and stitch the other crotch seam closed. Stitch over twice at casing to reinforce the seam.

Re-fold trousers into their finished form and stitch the inner leg seam closed.

Tie a sash around the waist, placing the knot at one side towards the front.

Sword

Cut one sword piece and two sheath pieces from leather or vinyl.

To make the sheath, glue along the side edges and press together. When the glue dries, place the sword in the sheath and tack it to one side under the sash.

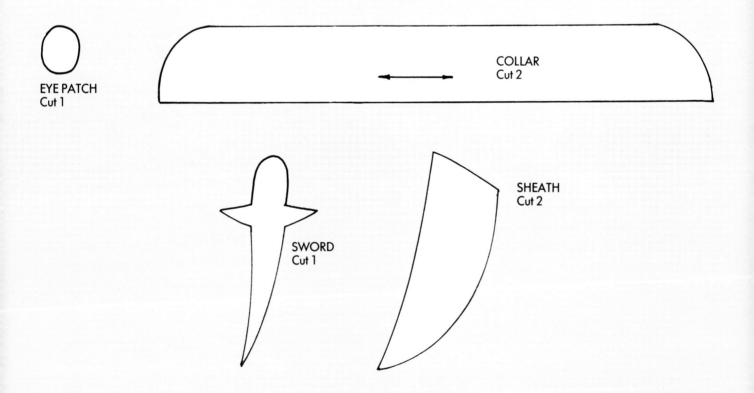

EYE PATCH
Cut 1

COLLAR
Cut 2

SWORD
Cut 1

SHEATH
Cut 2

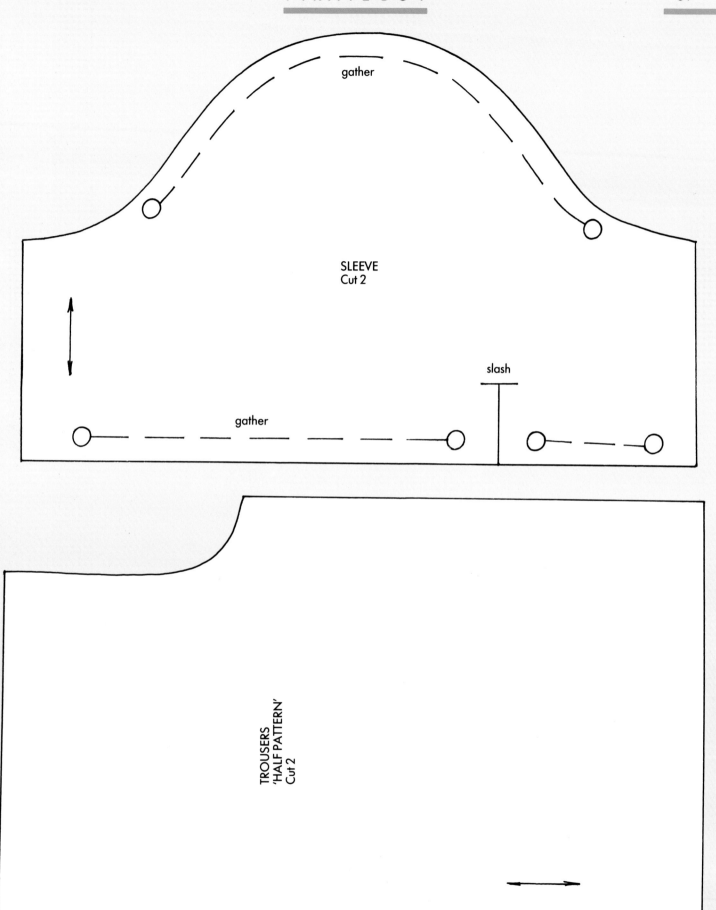

gather

SLEEVE
Cut 2

slash

gather

TROUSERS
'HALF PATTERN'
Cut 2

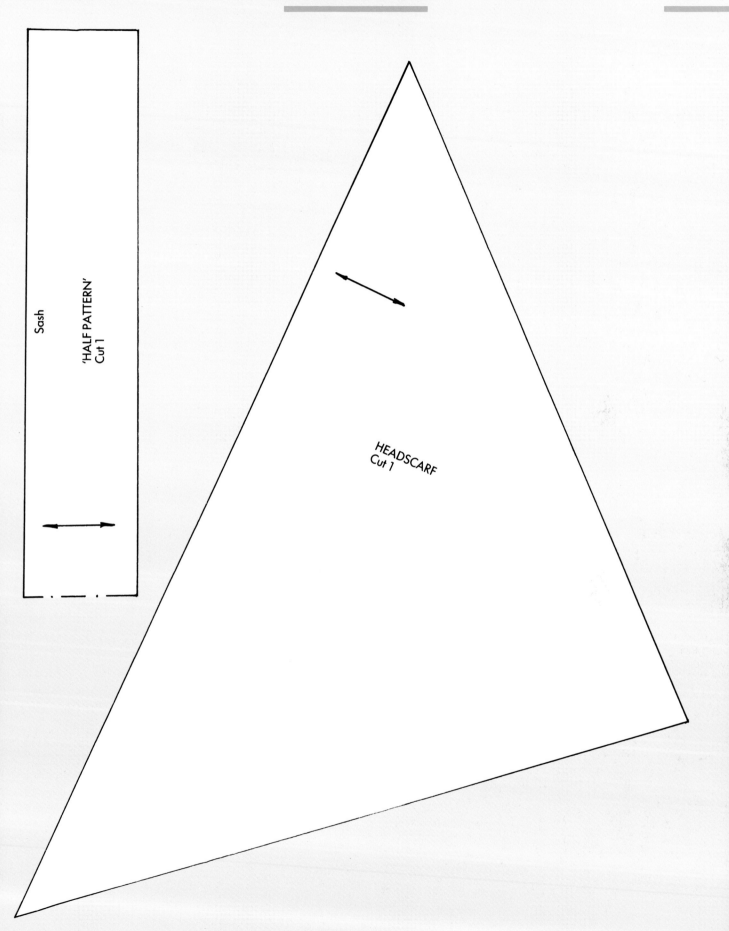

Sash

'HALF PATTERN'
Cut 1

HEADSCARF
Cut 1

PUNK BOY OR PUNK GIRL

MATERIALS

Earring small safety pin
Hair oddment of bright-coloured yarn
T-shirt 13 × 29 cm (5$^{1}/_{8}$ × 11$^{1}/_{2}$ in) jersey and 1 cm ($^{3}/_{8}$ in) sew-on fastening tape
Skirt 10 × 20 cm (4 × 8 in) tartan (girl)
Tights 18 × 20 cm (7 × 8 in) netting (girl)
Trousers 19 × 31 cm (7$^{1}/_{2}$ × 12$^{1}/_{4}$ in) tartan and 20 cm (8 in) narrow elastic (boy)
Jacket 12 × 58 cm (4$^{3}/_{4}$ × 22$^{7}/_{8}$ in) thin black vinyl; small safety pin; 8 cm (3$^{1}/_{4}$ in) small chain and a badge

INSTRUCTIONS

Doll's body

Girl: to make tights, cut two pieces out of netting using the pattern on page 16, and include them over the jersey when sewing legs.

Make the Basic Doll with ears (page 12) and shoes made of black vinyl.

It is important to start and finish off all facial feature threads at the back of the head in a vertical line up the middle, so that they can be concealed with the 'mohawk' hair.

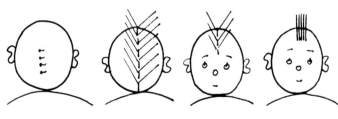

To make the Punk's mohawk, wind a strand of yarn 45 times or so around the hair card. Cut the wrapped yarn along the two folds, remove the cardboard and stitch up the middle of the head with small stitches for strength, and glue the two sections together in the middle.

Attach a small safety pin as an earring.

T-shirt (Girl or Boy)

Using the patterns on page 42, cut one front and two back bodices out of jersey.

Join the front bodice to the back bodice sections at the shoulders.

Turn under back opening with stitching and sew strips of fastening tape for closure.

Sew the side seam of the T-shirt.

Skirt (Girl)

Cut the piece of tartan in half, to get two 10 cm (4 in) squares of fabric. Turn under with stitching at the top and bottom of each piece. Now stitch along side seams, rounding them off at one end to form the waist, and turn right side out.

Trousers (Boy)

Cut two trouser pieces from tartan. Hem the bottom edges on each piece, and then stitch the two pieces together along one crotch seam only.

Open the joined piece flat and make a casing at the waist.

Thread a piece of elastic through with a safety pin. Stretch the elastic to fit the doll's waist and secure.

Fold the trousers in half and stitch the other crotch seam closed. Stitch over twice at casing to reinforce the seam.

Re-fold trousers into their finished form and stitch the inner leg seam closed.

Jacket

Cut the pair of front bodices, one back bodice, sleeves and the lapels from vinyl.

Stitch lapels directly to the right sides of the front bodice sections.

Join the front bodice sections to the back bodice at the shoulders.

To set the sleeves into the armholes, lay the garment

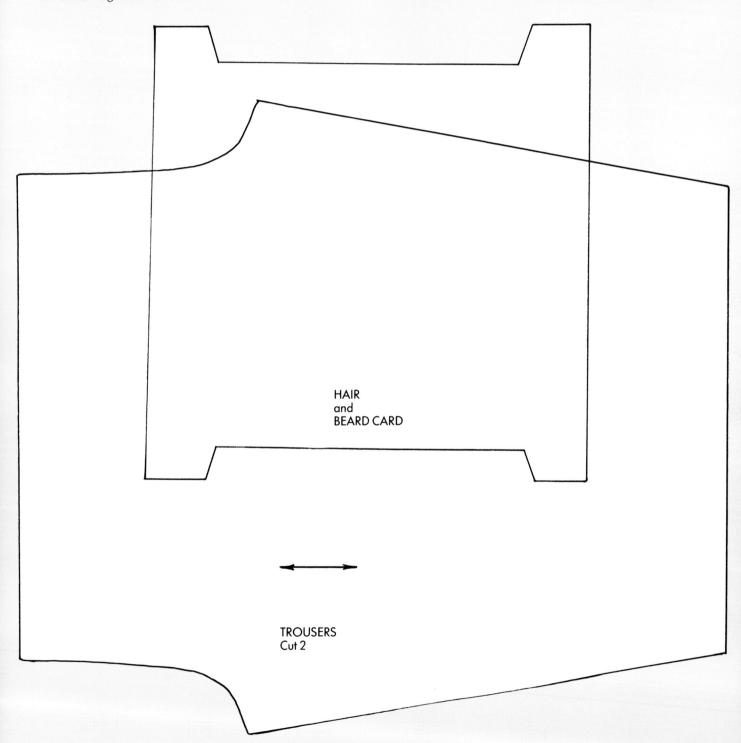

HAIR
and
BEARD CARD

TROUSERS
Cut 2

out flat and match the side edge of the bodice with the sleeve underarm edge. Pin the sleeve heads to the armholes and stitch over. Remove the pins.

Sew the underarm seam and the side seam of bodice in one operation.

Pull the ends of chain onto the safety pin and attach to the jacket. Pin the badge to the opposite side.

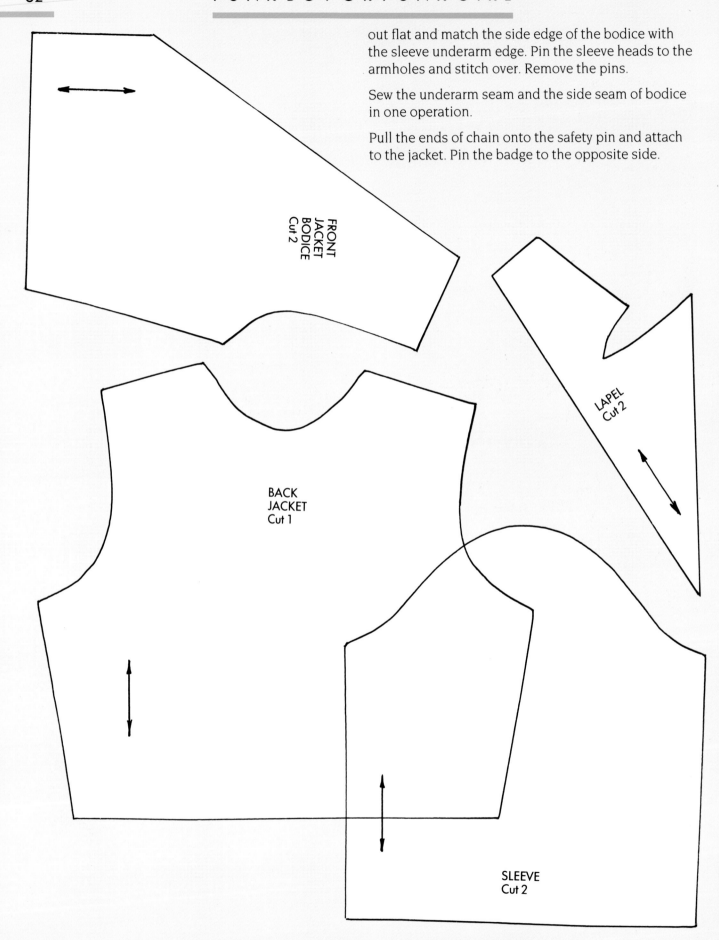

FRONT
JACKET
BODICE
Cut 2

LAPEL
Cut 2

BACK
JACKET
Cut 1

SLEEVE
Cut 2

AMERICAN INDIAN SQUAW

MATERIALS

Dress, headband, necklace and shoe fringe
16 × 74 cm (6³/₈ × 29¹/₈ in) thin leather; strong thread or yarn for hand stitching the pieces together and a small feather

INSTRUCTIONS

Doll's body

Make the Basic Doll (page 12) with long black hair and no socks.

To decorate the shoes, cut two fringe pieces and stitch or glue them at the back of the shoes to hold in place.

Dress

Cut one front and two back bodices, front and back skirts plus the sleeves from leather.

Use a cross-stitch for hand stitching the pieces together and also for decorating. (I used one colour for sewing the garment and another for decorating.)

Stitch the front bodice to the front skirt first, and then the back bodice sections to the back skirt. Now join the pieces together.

Lay the garment out flat and stitch in the sleeves.

Sew the underarm seam and the side seam of the dress in one operation.

Embroider a few cross-stitches up the back opening with a single strand of strong thread, leaving a bit at the ends dangling.

Headband

Cut a band out of leather and decorate it by embroidering a line of cross-stitches along it. Glue a small feather in the band to one side, and stitch or glue the band at the back of the head.

Necklace

Cut a 20 cm (8 in) thin strip and two circles each 2 cm (³/₄ in) in diameter out of leather.

Make a cross-stitch on one circle, catching the strip of leather in the middle with the same thread or yarn. Fasten off at the back.

Now spread a thin layer of glue on the wrong side and press onto the other circle. Place the necklace around the doll's neck and glue the ends of the strip together.

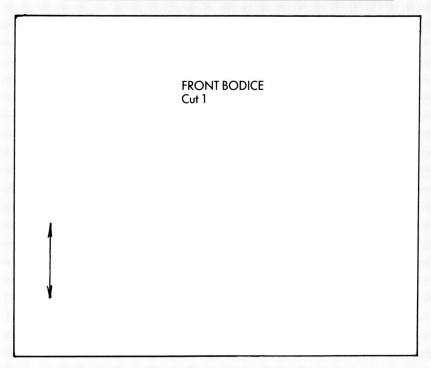

FRONT BODICE
Cut 1

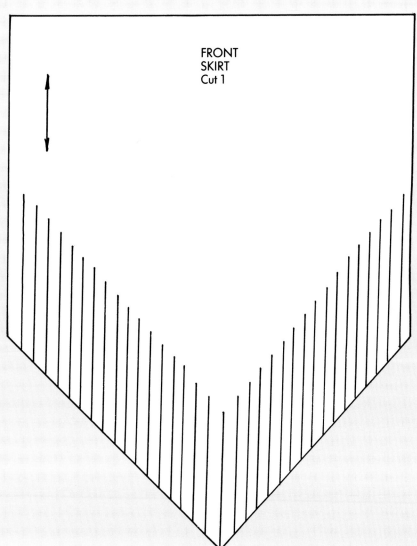

FRONT
SKIRT
Cut 1

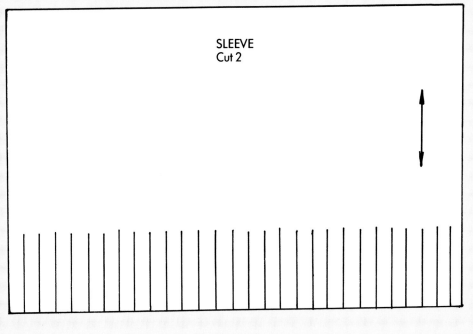

SLEEVE
Cut 2

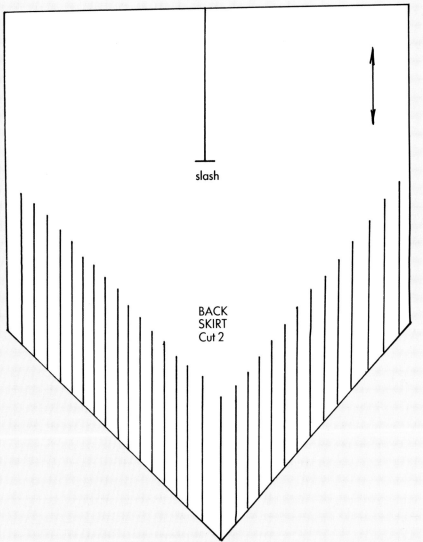

slash

BACK
SKIRT
Cut 2

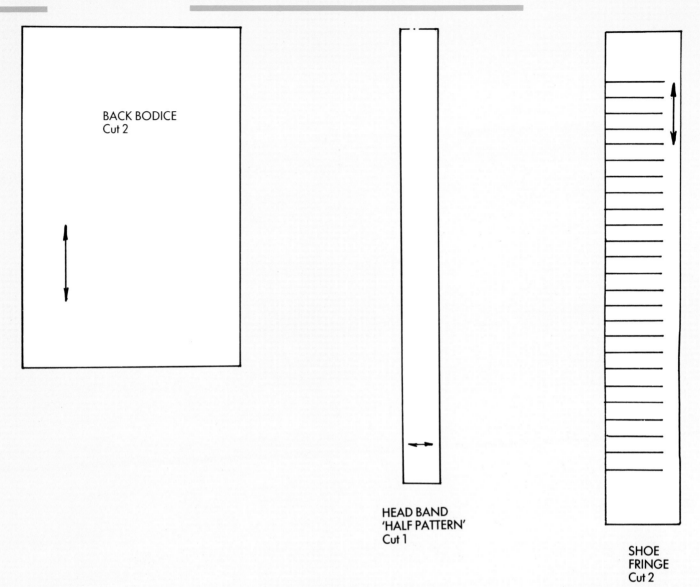

BACK BODICE
Cut 2

HEAD BAND
'HALF PATTERN'
Cut 1

SHOE
FRINGE
Cut 2

AFRICAN GIRL

MATERIALS

Hair decoration various small coloured beads
Underpants 9 × 30 cm (3½ × 11¾ in) plain light-weight fabric and 30 cm (11¾ in) narrow lace edging
Dress and headband 32 × 61 cm (12⅝ × 24 in) batik

INSTRUCTIONS

Doll's body

Make the Basic Doll (page 12) with long black hair (looped yarn is best to imitate curly hair) and no socks.

Decorate the hair by threading a few strands with various coloured beads.

Underpants

Using the pattern on page 40, cut two underpant pieces out of fabric.

Turn under 5 mm (¼ in) along the lower edges on each piece, place strips of lace edging onto the underside of the hem so that scalloped edge falls just below hemline and stitch.

Hem the waist edges and join pieces to each other by stitching along both crotch seams and then inner leg seams.

Dress

Cut a 18 × 61 cm (7⅛ × 24 in) rectangle, two 5 × 61 cm (2 × 24 in) strips and two shoulder straps out of fabric (page 53).

To make a frill, first join two strips of fabric together and then hem one long edge by turning it under with stitching. Sew two lines of gathering stitches along the other end and pull the gathers evenly to fit the bottom of the dress. Pin the frill to the dress and stitch. Remove the pins and then pull out the lower visible gathering thread.

Turn under 2 cm (¾ in) along the upper edge and sew three lines of gathering stitches, 1 cm (⅜ in) from the top and 1 cm (⅜ in) apart. Pull the fabric along the two threads, spreading the gathers evenly. Stitch, close to the gathering stitches to keep gathers in place, and remove the gathering threads.

Sew the side seam of the dress.

To make the shoulder straps, fold each strip of fabric in half lengthwise and stitch along the length. Trim the seam allowance to 2 mm (⅛ in), turn right-side out and press. Topstitch close to both edges if desired.

Stitch finished shoulder straps to inside of back waist, cross them over and stitch them to the inside of the front.

Headband

Cut a 4 × 61 cm (1⅝ × 24 in) strip of fabric, turn under both long edges and tie at the back of the head under the hair.

JAPANESE GIRL

MATERIALS

Underpants 9 × 30 cm (3$\frac{1}{2}$ × 11$\frac{3}{4}$ in) plain light-weight fabric and 30 cm (11$\frac{3}{4}$ in) narrow lace edging
Under-kimono 27 × 75 cm (10$\frac{5}{8}$ × 29$\frac{5}{8}$ in) plain light-weight fabric
Over-kimono and hair bow 27 × 75 cm (10$\frac{5}{8}$ × 29$\frac{5}{8}$ in) patterned light-weight fabric and 4 × 32 cm (1$\frac{5}{8}$ × 12$\frac{5}{8}$ in) plain light-weight fabric
Sash 4 × 43 cm (1$\frac{5}{8}$ × 17 in) plain or patterned light-weight fabric

INSTRUCTIONS

Doll's body

Make the Basic Doll (page 12) with long black hair and no socks.

When creating the eyes, snip at the bottom to create an Oriental look. Also, trim the hair short so it reaches the base of the neck.

Hair bow

Using the patterns on page 53, cut bow pieces out of fabric.

Stitch together two bow pieces leaving an opening through which to turn the right-side out. Trim the seam allowance, turn the right-side out, and slipstitch the opening closed.

Fold bow knot piece in half lengthwise and stitch along the length. Trim the seam allowance to 2 mm ($\frac{1}{8}$ in), turn right-side out and press. Topstitch close to both edges if desired.

Neatly pleat the bow by hand, then wrap the bow knot round and stitch it closed.

Stitch the bow at the top of the doll's head.

Underpants

Using the pattern on page 40, cut two underpant pieces out of fabric.

Turn under 5 mm ($\frac{1}{4}$ in) along the lower edges on each piece, place strips of lace edging on the underside of the hem so that the scalloped edge falls just below hemline and stitch.

Hem the waist edges and join pieces to each other by stitching along both crotch seams and then inner leg seams.

Under-kimono

There are two kimonos: one an undergarment and the other the top garment. Each is sewn with a lining.

Starting with the under-kimono, cut four front pieces (two for lining), two back pieces (one for lining), sleeves and collar out of the plain fabric.

Join a pair of front pieces to each of the two back pieces at the shoulders.

Fold the collar in half lengthwise and stitch to the neckline of one of the garments starting from the waist.

To join the lining, start sewing the two garments together at the front bottom edge, and follow around the neckline, making sure the collar has been flattened and sandwiched between the two, to end at the other front bottom edge. Side seams should not be stitched yet. Trim the seam allowance, turn right-side out and press.

Now lay out the garment flat and pin the sleeves at the shoulders, positioning the shoulder seam at the centre of the sleeve.

Fold the garment in half and start sewing at the sleeve ends where the curve begins (leaving hand opening unstitched), continuing down along the side edges of the garment.

Slipstitch the hem at the hand opening. Trim the seam allowance along the curve, turn right-side out and press.

Over-kimono

Cut four of the front pieces (two for lining), two of the back pieces (one for lining) and sleeves from patterned fabric plus collar from plain fabric.

Proceed in the same manner as for under-kimono.

Sash

Fold the strip of fabric in half lengthwise and stitch along the length leaving an opening for turning right-side out. Trim the seam allowance, turn right-side out, press and slipstitch the opening closed.

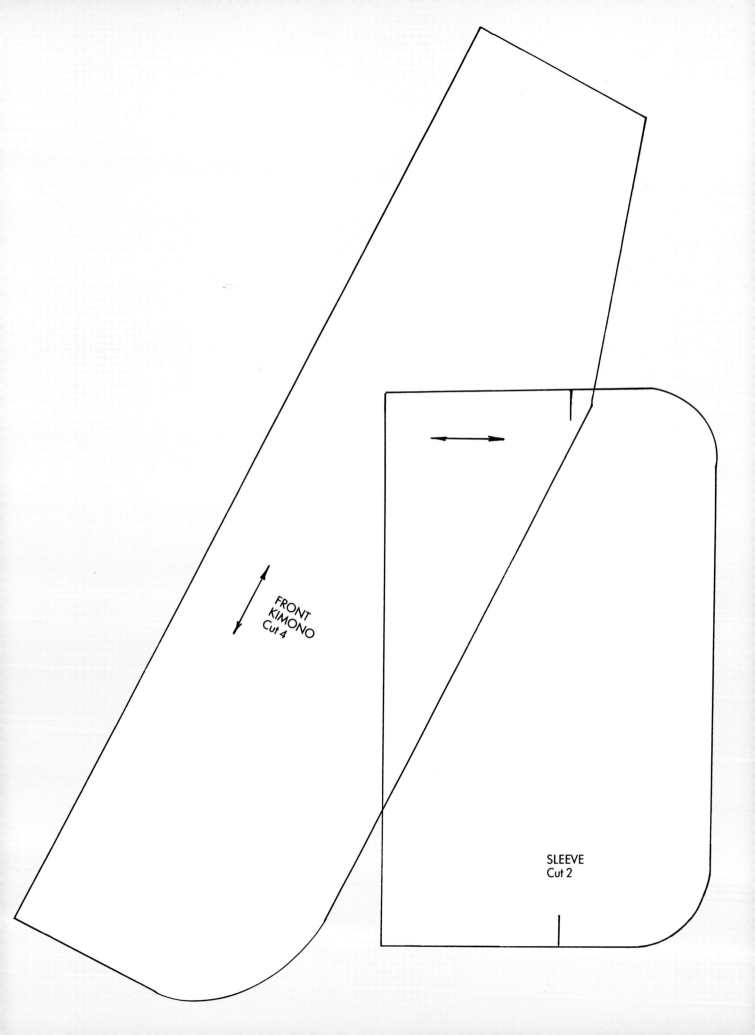

FRONT
KIMONO
Cut 4

SLEEVE
Cut 2

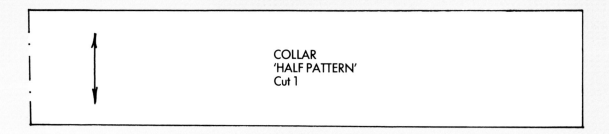

COLLAR
'HALF PATTERN'
Cut 1

BACK
KIMONO
'HALF PATTERN'
Cut 2

$\mathscr{I}$NDIAN $\mathscr{G}$IRL

MATERIALS

Underpants 9 × 30 cm (3½ × 11¾ in) plain light-weight fabric and 30 cm (11¾ in) narrow lace edging
Blouse 13 × 108 cm (5⅛ × 42½ in) plain light-weight fabric and 20 cm (8 in) narrow ribbon
Sari 20 × 120 cm (8 × 47¼ in) light-weight fabric with embroidered border

INSTRUCTIONS

Doll's body

Make the Basic Doll (page 12) with long black hair, no fringe and with no socks.

Make a parting at the front of the head and stitch the hair along the sides and back of the head just above the neckline and divide the hair at the back in two equal parts. Plait the strands at each side and tie off the ends with the same thread or yarn as used for the hair. Trim ends to even lengths on each plait.

Underpants

Using the pattern on page 40), cut two underpant pieces out of fabric.

Turn under 5 mm (¼ in) along the lower edges on each piece, place strips of lace edging on the underside of the hem so the scalloped edge falls just below hemline and stitch over.

Hem the waist edges and join pieces to each other by stitching along both crotch seams and then inner leg seams.

Blouse

Cut two of the front bodices (one for lining), four of the back bodices (two for lining) plus the four sleeves (two for lining) out of the fabric.

Join together the pair of front bodice pieces along the neck edge. Trim the seam allowance carefully to 2 mm (⅛ in), turn right-side out and press. Sandwich the four back pieces into two pairs, joining each along the neck edge and then along centre back. Trim the seam allowance, turn right-side out and press.

Join front bodice to back bodice at the shoulders.

Join the four sleeve pieces into two pairs by stitching them along lower edges. Trim the seam allowance, turn right-side out and press.

To set the sleeves into the armholes, lay out the garment flat and match the side edge of the bodice with the sleeve underarm edge. Pin the sleeve heads to the armholes and stitch. Remove the pins.

Sew 10 cm (4 in) strips of narrow ribbon to the back opening for closure.

Hem the bottom edge of the blouse.

Sari

This garment consists of a length of light-weight cloth draped over the body so that one end forms a skirt and the other a head or shoulder covering.

Start wrapping the fabric at the doll's waist from right to left, and around the back, bringing it to the front again. At the centre of the front hand stitch four even pleats, continuing the fabric around the back again.

When you meet up at the original point where the fabric started (the right side of the waist), gather the remainder in a neat bunch at the waist and fling it up over the left shoulder.

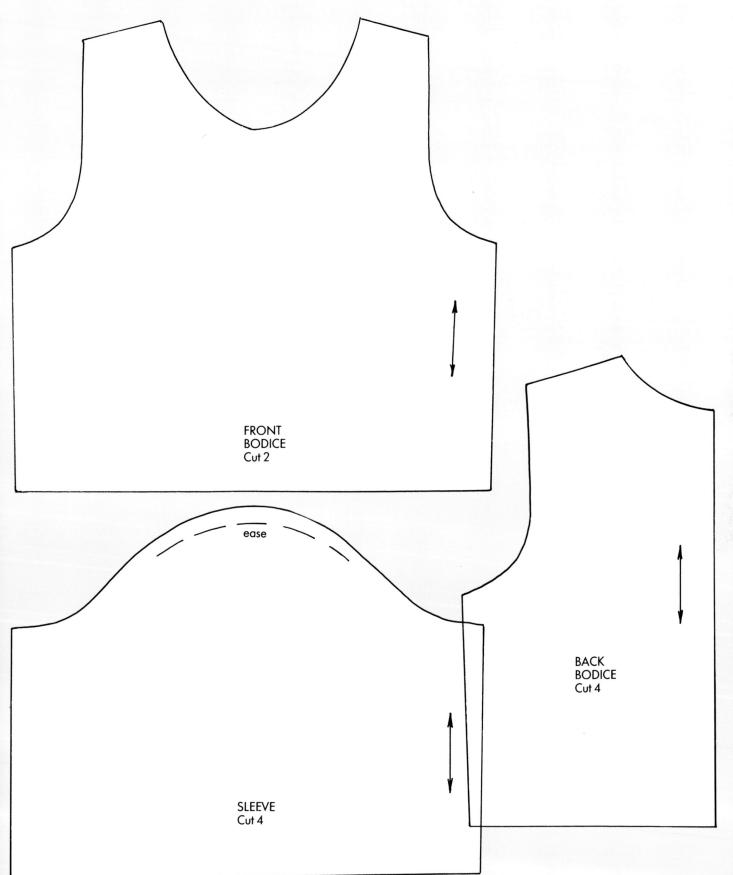

FRONT
BODICE
Cut 2

ease

SLEEVE
Cut 4

BACK
BODICE
Cut 4

$\mathcal{S}$NOW $\mathcal{W}$HITE

MATERIALS

Hair bows 20 cm (8 in) narrow ribbon
Underpants 9 × 30 cm (3½ × 11¾ in) plain light-weight fabric and 30 cm (11¾ in) narrow lace edging
Dress 25 × 64 cm (9⅞ × 25¼ in) yellow light-weight fabric; 10 × 86 cm (4 × 33⅞ in) blue light-weight fabric; 3 × 25 cm (1⅛ × 9⅞ in) white light-weight fabric; 25 cm (9⅞ in) black thread and 20 cm (8 in) narrow ribbon

INSTRUCTIONS

Doll's body

Make the Basic Doll (page 12) with long black hair and no socks.

To make plaits, stitch the hair along the back and sides of the head just above the neckline and divide the hair in two equal parts at the nape. Plait the strands of each side and tie off the ends with the same thread or yarn as used for the hair. Trim ends to even lengths on each plait.

Make two ribbon bows by cutting the piece of ribbon in half and crossing the ends. Stitch around the middle with a thread of the same colour. Apply a thin layer of glue to the ends and trim them when dry.

Stitch the bows to the end of each plait.

Underpants

Using the pattern on page 40, cut two underpant pieces out of fabric.

Turn under 5 mm (¼ in) along the lower edges on each

piece, place strips of lace edging on the underside of the hem so that scalloped edge falls just below hemline and stitch.

Hem the waist edges and join the pieces to each other by stitching along both crotch seams and then inner leg seams.

Dress

Cut 15 × 61 cm (5⅞ × 24 in) rectangle, two 5 × 61 cm (2 × 24 in) strips and sleeve bands from yellow fabric. Cut two of front bodices (one for lining), four of back bodices (two for lining) and sleeves out of blue fabric.

Join the pair of front bodices together along the neck edge. Trim the seam allowance carefully to 2 mm (⅛ in). Turn right-side out and press. Join the two pairs of back bodice sections along the neck edge and then along centre back. Trim the seam allowance, turn right-side out and press.

Join the front bodice piece to the back bodice sections at the shoulders.

Make short, full sleeves with bands. First sew two parallel lines of gathering stitches around the sleeve heads and then along the bottom edge, 1 cm (⅜ in) apart and between the dots indicated on the pattern. Pull the gathers evenly to fit the armholes. To join the sleeves to the rest of the dress, stitch the seam through the middle of the two gathered rows, remove the pins and then pull out the lower visible gathering thread. Now pull the fabric along the two threads on the bottom of the sleeves to fit the width of the bands. Fold the band pieces in half lengthwise, pin over the gathering and stitch. Remove the pins and pull out the lower visible gathering thread.

Sew the underarm seam and the side seam of bodice in one operation.

To construct the skirt, first make a frill by joining the strips of fabric to form a long strip. Hem one long edge by turning it under with stitching. Now gather the other end and pull the gathers evenly to fit the bottom of the dress. Pin the frill to the dress and stitch over. Remove the pins and then pull out the lower visible gathering thread.

Now gather the waist edge of the skirt to fit the lower edge of bodice.

Join the edges of the skirt, beginning the stitch from the hemmed edge of the frill and up to within 4 cm (1½ in) of the waist edge. Spread the seam and stitch along the V-opening to form a hem.

Now pin the gathered waist edge of the skirt to the waist edge of the bodice and stitch through the middle of the gathered rows, remove the pins and pull out the lower visible gathering thread.

Embroider a few cross-stitches up the front bodice with a black thread.

Fold the piece of white fabric in half lengthwise and make equal pleats all along, pinning them in place. Hand stitch to the inside of the front bodice along the neckline to form ruffle.

Cut 20 cm (8 in) piece of ribbon in half and stitch two strips to the back opening for closure.

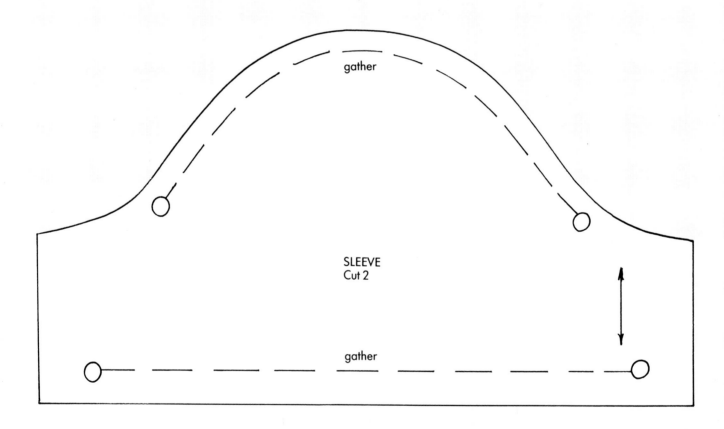

SLEEVE
Cut 2

gather

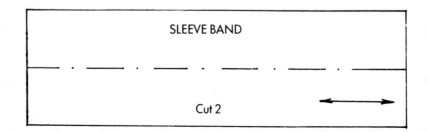

SLEEVE BAND

Cut 2

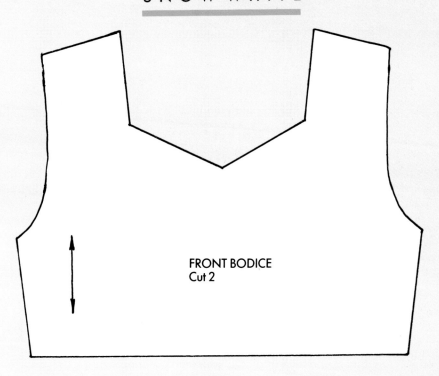

FRONT BODICE
Cut 2

The Seven Dwarfs

MATERIALS REQUIRED FOR EACH DWARF

Body and legs 25 × 84 cm (9⁷⁄₈ × 33¹⁄₈ in) flesh-coloured jersey

Stuffing 100 g (4 oz) white polyester

Facial features 1 × 2 cm (³⁄₈ × ³⁄₄ in) black vinyl; 91 cm (36 in) strand of flesh-coloured crochet thread; 30 cm (11³⁄₄ in) strand of red crochet thread and 50 cm (19³⁄₄ in) strand of white crochet thread

Beard (except Dopey) 25 g (1 oz) thick white yarn

Glasses (Doc only) 30 cm (11³⁄₄ in) picture wire

Jacket 14 × 56 cm (5¹⁄₂ × 22¹⁄₈ in) plain light-weight fabric; 20 cm (8 in) narrow bias tape and two large buttons

Trousers 14 × 32 cm (5¹⁄₂ × 12⁵⁄₈ in) plain light-weight fabric and 20 cm (8 in) narrow elastic

Patches 5 cm (2 in) square of patterned light-weight fabric for each one

Hat and shoes 16 × 54 cm (6³⁄₈ × 21¹⁄₄ in) plain medium-weight fabric

INSTRUCTIONS

Doll's body

Trace the full Body pattern (page 88), or Body with ears if making Dopey (page 89), onto two layers of jersey, making sure the grain of the fabric is vertical.

Turn up 2 cm (³⁄₄ in) hem around lower edge and sew with a small stitch all around, following the traced marks. It is important to stretch the jersey slightly when sewing so the seams do not snap when the doll is stuffed.

> I have not included the seam allowance on the Body pattern piece so that you can accurately stitch the doll form. It is therefore necessary that you form your own seam allowance after sewing by cutting the fabric carefully 1 cm (³⁄₈ in) away from the seam line. Clip the curves.

Legs

Cut four leg pieces out of jersey.

Join each pair by stitching all sides except the top.

Stuffing

Turn right sides of body and leg pieces out using a large screwdriver, being careful not to puncture the jersey.

First stuff the head and neck firmly using a little of the stuffing at a time to mould firm and smooth surfaces. Then stuff the rest of the body and legs, paying careful attention to the contours you are forming.

Don't stuff all the way to the brim of each opening, but leave 2 cm (³⁄₄ in) unfilled.

If making Dopey (when ears are included), make sure to sew 1 cm (³⁄₈ in) into each ear from top and bottom and take special care when bringing their shape out to achieve a curled look. Leave the ears empty when stuffing the rest of the body.

Neck

First choose the smoother side of the head for the face. To form the neck, use a long darning needle and a single flesh-coloured crochet thread. Start the thread at the back of the head on the neckline and wrap it twice around the front. Pull it tightly to create a neck, and fasten off at the back of the head.

Joining the legs to the body

Push the tops of the legs into the opening on the lower body, making sure that the toes are pointing towards the front.

Use a long darning needle and single flesh-coloured thread and sew across the torso opening with a small stitch from one end to the other. It is important to stitch this point of the doll securely, as it is the weakest point on the body.

FACIAL FEATURES

Mouth

Start a doubled red crochet thread at the back of the head, push the darning needle through to the front and embroider a different mouth for each dwarf (see the illustration). Fasten off the thread at the back of the head.

Nose

Use 4 cm (1½ in) square of jersey, a fine needle, doubled ordinary sewing thread, and a wad of stuffing, and make a nose as for Basic Doll (page 14).

Using a cross-stitch coming through from the back of the head, sew the nose to the face. To reinforce it further, dab a little glue under the loose edges of the nose.

Eyes (except Sleepy)

Cut two eye circles (one if making Grumpy) out of vinyl with a leather- or paper-punch.

Start a single white crochet thread at the back of the head and push the darning needle through to the face. Measure 1 cm (³⁄₈ in) out from the sides of the nose and then 1 cm (³⁄₈ in) up, and bring out the needle at this point.

Puncture eye circle through the upper middle with the needle and return the thread through the face just above the eye, and fasten off at the back.

If making Grumpy, embroider an eyelid instead of one eye.

Eyelashes (Sleepy and Bashful)

Using an ordinary black thread, embroider a few stitches for eyelashes, starting and fastening the thread off at the back of the head.

Eyebrows

Using an ordinary black sewing thread or a white thick yarn, embroider lines in an angle suggesting eyebrows (see illustration), starting and fastening off the thread or yarn at the back of the head.

Cheeks

Using a pale shade of make-up rouge, apply a small quantity lightly to the doll's cheeks and to the nose if making Bashful.

Beard

Using the pattern on page 61, wind a yarn around it. Cut the wrapped yarn off the card with a single straight cut, lay it out flat, and then stitch through the middle.

Take the end strands to each side behind the ear, bringing them together at the back of the head, and stitch in place. Fold the beard in half at the seam line, then hand stitch it round the face just under the chin.

Unravel individual strands of yarn with a fine-tooth comb for fullness and trim the beard to required length.

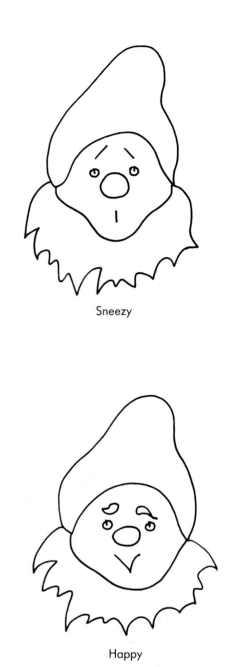

Doc

Bashful

Sneezy

Sleepy

Grumpy

Happy

Dopey

Glasses

Take the piece of picture wire and wind it around a pen or pencil once 10 cm (4 in) from one end, forming a circle. Leave a small gap and make another circle in the same way. Adjust the length of the ends, and hand stitch the glasses at the sides of the head.

Jacket

Cut two front bodice pieces, one back bodice and sleeves out of fabric.

Sew the shoulder seams of the front bodice sections to the back bodice and turn under the front opening with stitching to form facings.

Hem the lower edges of the sleeves by turning them under with stitching. To set them into the armholes, lay the garment out flat and match the side edge of the bodice with the sleeve underarm edge. Pin the sleeve heads to the armholes and stitch over. Remove the pins.

Sew the underarm seam and the side seam of bodice in one operation.

Turn under the front openings with stitching to form facings.

To bind the neck edge unfold one raw edge of the binding tape, place it to the right side of the jacket (with bias tape edge level with the neck edge), and stitch along the crease of the binding. Fold the other pressed edge of bias tape to the wrong side of the jacket, turn in the ends on each side and slipstitch along the hem.

Hem the jacket by turning under the bottom edge with stitching and sew on the buttons for fastening.

Trousers

Cut two of the trouser pieces out of fabric.

Hem the bottom edges on each trouser piece, and then stitch the two pieces together along one crotch seam only.

Open joined piece flat and make a casing at the waist. Thread a piece of elastic through with a safety pin. Stretch the elastic to fit the doll's waist and secure.

Fold the trousers in half and stitch the other crotch seam closed. Stitch over twice at casing to reinforce the seam.

Re-fold trousers into their finished form and stitch the inner leg seam closed.

Cap

Cut one cap piece out of fabric.

Turn under the bottom edge with stitching. Join the side seam, trim the seam allowance and turn right side out.

Boots

Cut two boot pieces out of fabric.

Fold each piece in half and stitch along all sides except the top. Trim the seam allowance and turn right-side out.

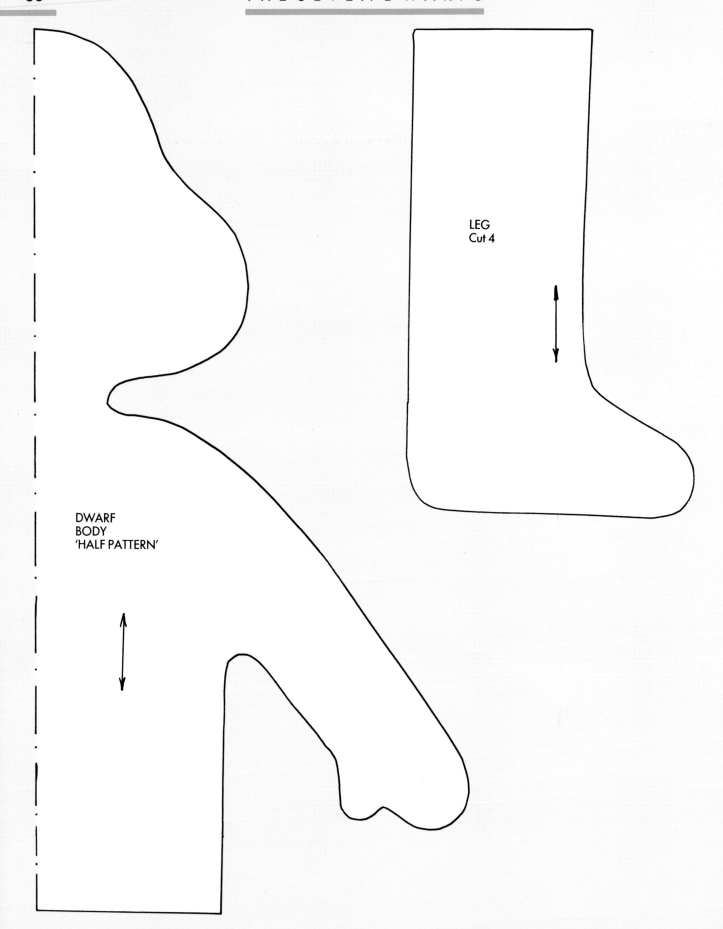

LEG
Cut 4

DWARF
BODY
'HALF PATTERN'

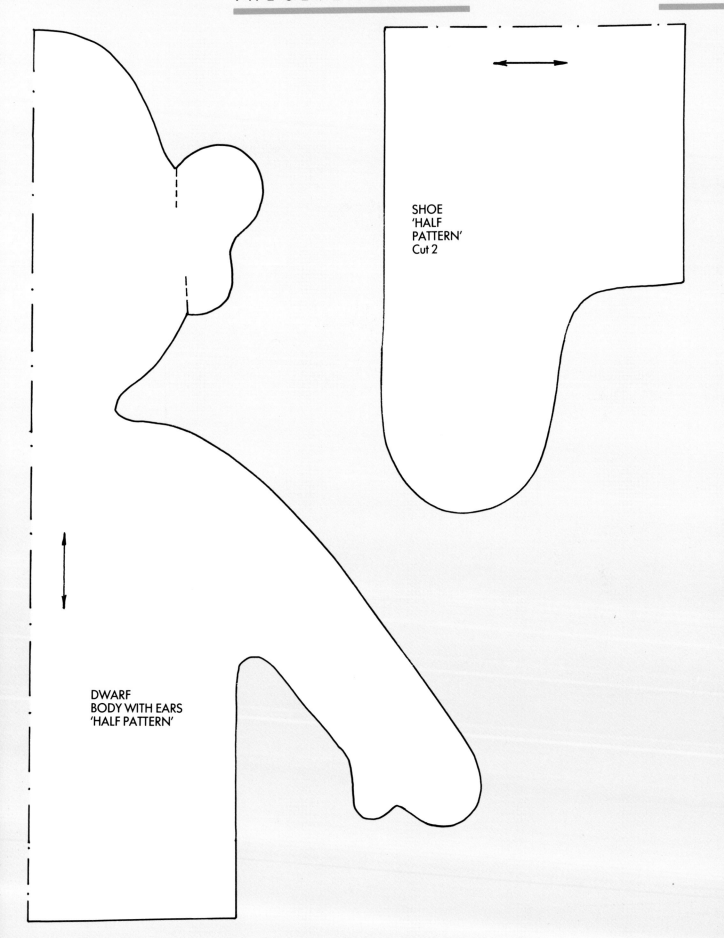

SHOE
'HALF
PATTERN'
Cut 2

DWARF
BODY WITH EARS
'HALF PATTERN'

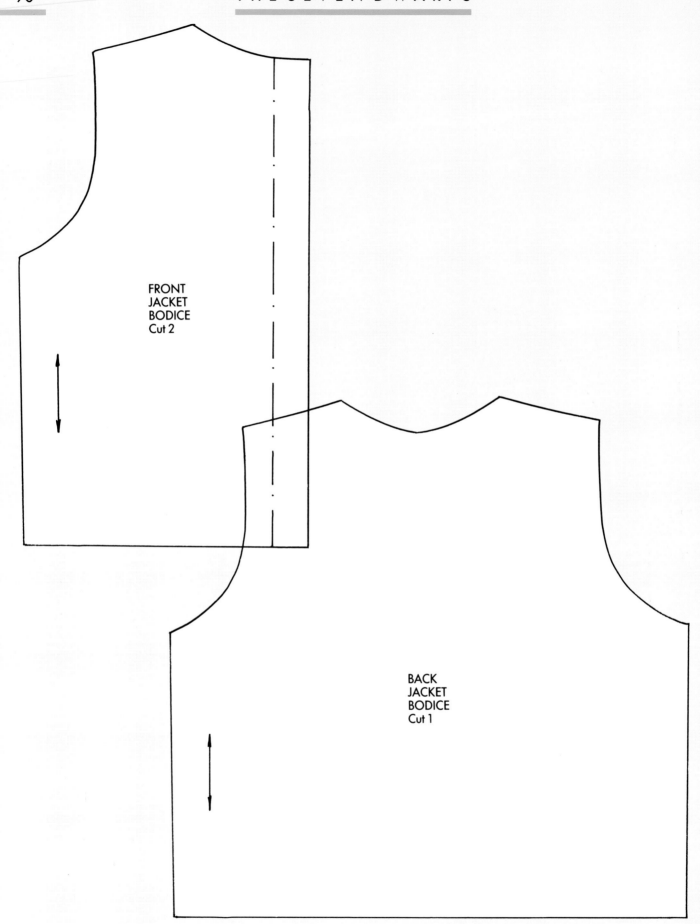

FRONT
JACKET
BODICE
Cut 2

BACK
JACKET
BODICE
Cut 1

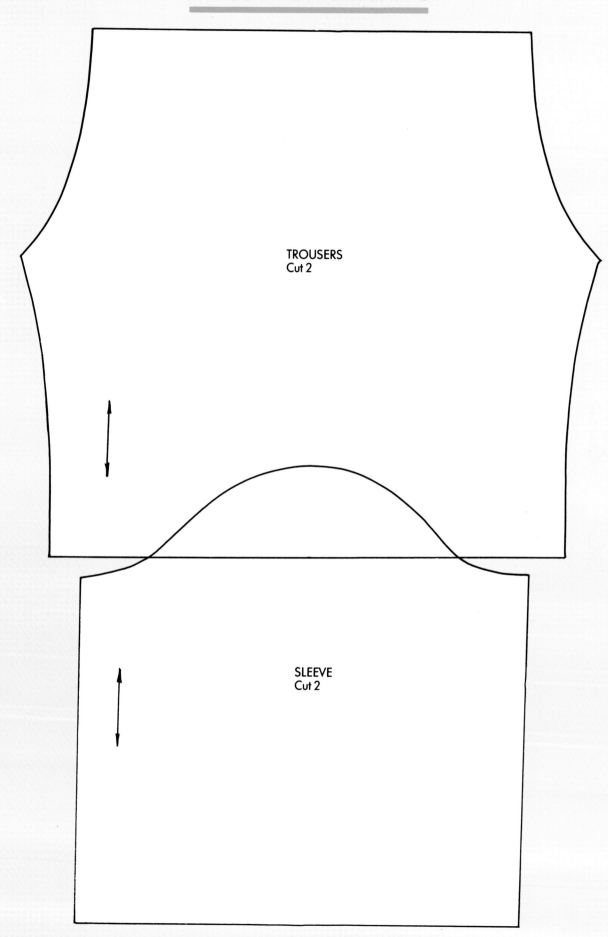

TROUSERS
Cut 2

SLEEVE
Cut 2

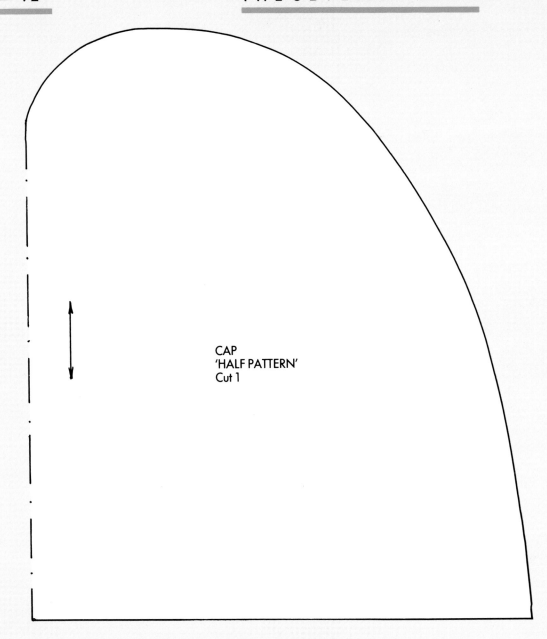

CAP
'HALF PATTERN'
Cut 1

HEIDI

MATERIALS

Shoelaces 61 cm (24 in) strand of strong yarn or thread

Hair bows 20 cm (8 in) narrow ribbon

Underpants 9 × 30 cm (3½ × 11¾ in) plain light-weight fabric and 30 cm (11¾ in) narrow lace edging

Dress 33 × 61 cm (13 × 24 in) checked light-weight fabric; 13 × 78 cm (5⅛ × 30¾ in) plain light-weight fabric; 20 cm (8 in) narrow elastic; 30 cm (11¾ in) narrow lace edging; 20 cm (8 in) narrow ribbon and 1 cm (⅜ in) sew-on fastening tape

INSTRUCTIONS

Doll's body

Make the Basic Doll (page 12) with long blonde hair and knee-socks.

To make plaits, stitch the hair along the back and sides of the head just above the neckline and divide the hair in two equal parts at the nape. Plait the strands of each side and tie off the ends with the same thread or yarn as used for the hair. Trim ends to even lengths on each plait.

Make two ribbon bows by cutting the piece of ribbon in half and crossing the ends. Stitch around the middle with a thread of the same colour. Apply a thin layer of glue to the ends, trim when dry and stitch the bows to the end of each plait.

Embroider a few cross-stitches on the front of the shoes for laces.

Underpants

Using the pattern on page 40 cut two underpant pieces out of fabric.

Turn under 5 mm (¼ in) along the lower edges on each piece, place strips of lace edging on the underside of the hem so that the scalloped edge falls just below hemline and stitch.

Hem the waist edges and join pieces to each other by stitching along both crotch seams and then inner leg seams.

Dress

Using patterns on pages 42 and 24, cut one of front bodice, two of back bodices and sleeves from plain fabric. Also, cut two of the front bib pieces (one for lining), four of back bib pieces (two for lining), a 13 × 61 cm (5⅛ × 24 in) rectangle and two 5 × 61 cm (2 × 24 in) strips out of checked fabric.

Join a pair of front bib pieces along the neck edge and sides. Trim the seam allowance carefully to 2 mm (⅛ in), turn right-side out and press.

Join the four back bib pieces into two pairs along the neck edge and then along the centre back and sides.

Trim the seam allowance, turn right-side out; press.

Pin the front bib over the front bodice of the dress, and the two back bib pieces over the two back bodice sections of the dress.

Sew the shoulder seams of the fronts to the backs.

Make short full sleeves with frills by turning up a 2 cm (¾ in) deep hem at the sleeve ends and stitching a 10 cm (4 in) piece of elastic along with the hem. Stretch the elastic to fit as you sew.

Sew two lines of gathering stitches around the sleeve heads 1 cm ($^3/_8$ in) apart and between dots indicated on the pattern. Pull the gathers evenly to fit the armholes. Lay out the garment flat and match side edge of bodice with sleeve underarm edge. Pin the sleeve heads to the armholes. To join sleeves to the rest of the bodice, stitch the seam through the middle of the two gathered rows, remove the pins and then pull out the lower visible gathering thread.

Sew underarm seam and side seam of bodice in one operation.

To construct the skirt, first make a frill by joining two strips of fabric to form a long strip. Hem one long edge by turning it under with stitching. Now gather the frill 1 cm ($^3/_8$ in) from one long edge, pulling the gathers to fit the bottom edge of the skirt. Pin and stitch between the two rows of gathering threads. Remove the pins and pull out the lower visible gathering thread.

Now gather the waist edge of the skirt to fit the lower edge of the bodice and pin. Stitch through the middle of the gathered rows, remove the pins and pull out the lower visible gathering thread.

Join the edges of the skirt, beginning to stitch from the hemmed edge of the frill and up to within 4 cm ($1^1/_2$ in) of the waist edge taking a 1 cm ($^3/_8$ in) seam. Spread the entire back seam and stitch along the V-opening to form a hem.

Sew strips of fastening tape to back bodice sections of the dress and strips of ribbon to the tops of back bib bodices for closure.

To make the lace collar, hem raw edges on each short side of lace strip. Gather one long edge to fit the neck, pin and stitch it to the right side of the dress. Remove the pins, then press the neck seam towards the dress and topstitch the hem under the collar to hold in place.

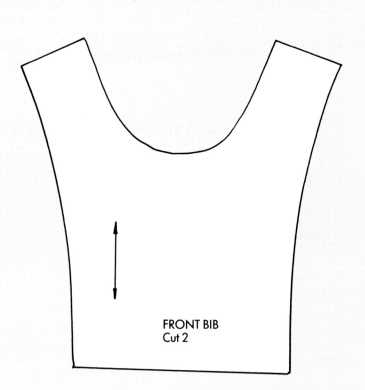

FRONT BIB
Cut 2

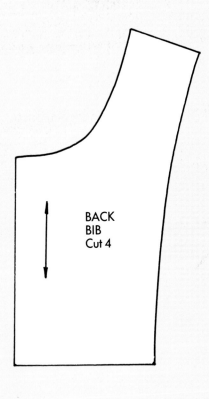

BACK
BIB
Cut 4

PETER

MATERIALS

Shoelaces 61 cm (24 in) strand of strong yarn or thread

Shirt 15 × 65 cm (6 × 25⅝ in) plain light-weight fabric and 8 cm (3¼ in) sew-on fastening tape 5 mm (¼ in) width

Shorts 17 × 34 cm (6¾ × 13½ in) plain medium-weight fabric and two small buttons

Hat 19 × 21 cm (7½ × 8¼ in) felt and one small feather

INSTRUCTIONS

Doll's body

Make the Basic Doll (page 12) closing the head gap to add short hair later, and including knee-socks.

Embroider a few cross-stitches with a single strand of yarn or thread on the front of the shoes for laces.

Shirt

Using the patterns on pages 33–4, cut one back bodice, two of front bodices, sleeves, cuffs and collar pieces out of plain fabric.

Sew the shoulder seams of the front bodice sections to the back bodice and turn under the front opening with stitching to form facings.

Slash and hem the sleeve openings and make pleats at the wrist ends as indicated on the pattern. To make cuffs, stitch the four pieces together into two pairs around the curved edges, carefully trim the seam allowance to 2 mm (⅛ in), turn right-side out and press.

To set the seams into the armholes, sew two lines of gathering stitches around sleeve heads 1 cm (⅜ in) apart, between dots indicated on the pattern, and pull the gathers to ease the sleeve crowns. Lay the garment out flat and match the side edge of the bodice with the sleeve underarm edge. Pin the sleeve heads to the armholes. Stitch, remove the pins, and pull out visible gathering thread.

Sew the underarm seam and the side seam of bodice in one operation.

Attach the cuffs to the wrist end of the sleeves from one slash to the other. Sew 5 mm (¼ in) piece of fastening tape to each cuff for closure.

Make a shirt collar by stitching the two pieces together around the outer edges, trim the seam allowance to 2 mm (⅛ in), turn right-side out and press. Stitch one side of the collar's neck edge to the outside neck edge of the shirt. Slipstitch the other side of the collar to the inside of the neckline. Top-stitch along the dotted line on the collar to form a foldline.

Hem the shirt by turning it under with stitching.

Sew the remaining piece of fastening tape along the facings on the front of the short (I sewed the tape on here with a zigzag stitch, giving the garment a decorative appearance).

Shorts

Cut two shorts pieces (page 20) plus two shoulder straps (page 98) out of fabric.

Hem the top and bottom of each piece, sew along both crotch seams and then inner leg seams.

To make shoulder straps, fold each strip of fabric in half lengthwise and stitch along the length, closing one end of each. Trim the seam allowance to 2 mm (⅛ in), turn right-side out and press. Topstitch close to both edges if desired.

Stitch finished shoulder straps to inside of back waist, cross them over and stitch them to the outside of the front. Sew on the buttons.

Hat

Cut all hat pieces out of felt. Stitch the brim piece to the side edge of the hat. Join the side seams together. Stitch in the crown.

Glue a small feather to one side of the hat.

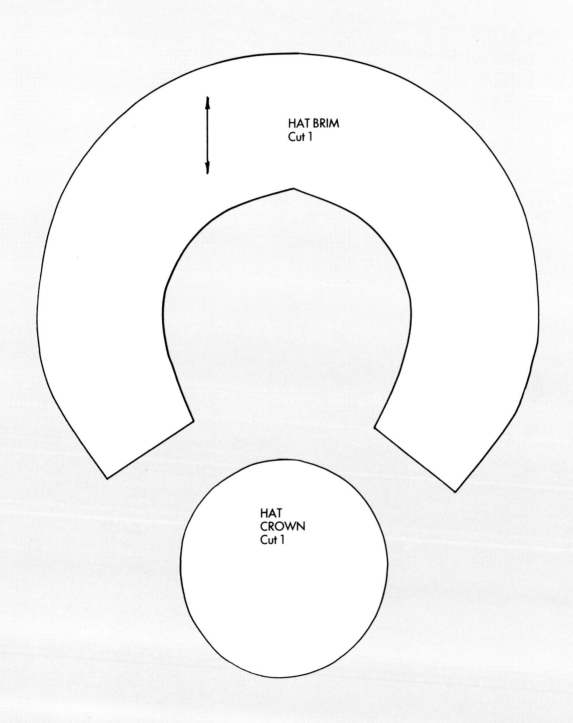

HAT BRIM
Cut 1

HAT
CROWN
Cut 1

HAT
SIDE
Cut 1

SHOULDER
STRAP

Cut 2

GRANDMA

MATERIALS

Wrinkles 30 cm (11³/₄ in) strand of flesh-coloured crochet thread

Glasses 30 cm (11³/₄ in) picture wire

Drawers and petticoat 20 × 95 cm (8 × 37³/₈ in) plain light-weight fabric; 40 cm (15³/₄ in) narrow elastic and 95 cm (37¹/₂ in) narrow lace edging

Dress 34 × 62 cm (13³/₈ × 24¹/₂ in) patterned light-weight fabric; 20 cm (8 in) narrow elastic; 7 × 26 cm (2³/₄ × 10¹/₄ in) plain light-weight fabric and 1 cm (³/₈ in) sew-on fastening tape

Apron and cap 20 × 75 cm (8 × 29¹/₂ in) plain light-weight fabric; 31 cm (12¹/₄ in) lace edging and 20 cm (8 in) narrow elastic

INSTRUCTIONS

Doll's body

Make the Basic Doll (page 12) with long white hair, no fringe and including ankle-socks.

Embroider the wrinkles on the face starting the flesh-coloured thread at the back of the head. Take it through to the front coming out just beside the nose, and then back through at the base of the neck. Pull the thread tightly to form wrinkles and finish them off at the back of the head.

Glasses

Take the piece of picture wire and wind it around a pen or pencil once 10 cm (4 in) from one end, forming a circle. Leave a small gap and make another circle in the same way. Adjust the length of the ends, and hand stitch the glasses at the sides of the head.

Drawers

Cut two drawer pieces (page 20) out of plain fabric. Turn under 5 mm (¹/₄ in) along the lower edges and place the strips of lace edging on the underside of the hem on each drawer piece so that the scalloped edge falls just below the hemline. Stitch.

Now join the drawer pieces to each other by stitching along one crotch seam only. Open the joined piece flat and make a casing at the waist. Thread a 20 cm (8 in) piece of elastic through with a safety pin. Stretch the elastic to fit the doll's waist and secure.

Fold the drawers in half and stitch the other crotch seam closed. Stitch over twice at casing to reinforce the seam. Re-fold drawers into their finished form and stitch the inner leg seam closed.

Petticoat

Cut a 20 cm × 61 cm (8 in × 24 in) rectangle from the plain fabric.

Turn under 5 mm (¹/₄ in) along the lower edge and place the raw edge of the lace on the underside of the hem so that the scalloped edge falls just below the hemline. Stitch. Make a casing on the other long edge. Thread a 20 cm (8 in) piece of elastic through the casing with a safety pin. Stretch the elastic to fit the doll's waist and secure.

Fold the petticoat in half and stitch the side seam closed. Stitch over twice at casing to reinforce the seam.

Dress

Cut one front, two back bodices, and a 20 × 61 cm (8 × 24 in) rectangle from patterned fabric. Also using cut four collar pieces out of plain fabric and sleeves from patterned fabric (pages 22–4).

Sew the shoulder seams of the front bodice to the back bodice sections.

Make long full sleeves with frills by hemming the sleeve ends and stitching 10 cm (4 in) piece of elastic 1 cm (³⁄₈ in) from the hemmed edge. Stretch the elastic to fit as you sew.

Sew two lines of gathering stitches around the sleeve heads 1 cm (³⁄₈ in) apart and between dots indicated on the pattern. Pull the gathers evenly to fit the armholes. Lay out the garment flat and match side edge of bodice with sleeve underarm edge. Pin the sleeve heads to the armholes. To join sleeves to the rest of the dress, stitch the seam through the middle of the two gathered rows, remove pins and then pull out the lower visible gathering thread.

Sew underarm seam and side seam of the dress in one operation.

Hem the bottom of the skirt by turning it under with stitching.

Now gather the waist edge of the skirt to fit the lower edge of bodice and pin. Stitch through the middle of the gathered rows, remove the pins and pull out the lower visible thread.

Join the edges of the skirt, beginning to stitch from the hemmed edge and up to within 4 cm (1¹⁄₂ in) of the waist edge taking a 1 cm (³⁄₈ in) seam. Spread the entire back seam and stitch along the V-opening to form a hem. Sew strips of fastening tape at the top of the back opening for easy dressing.

To make the collar, stitch together the four pieces into two pairs along their outer edges. Trim the seam allowance carefully to 2 mm (¹⁄₈ in), turn right-side out, press and pin to the neck edge of the right side of the dress, easing the curves one into the other. Stitch, remove pins and then press the neck seam towards the dress and topstitch the hem under the collar to hold in place.

Apron

Cut a 16 × 31 cm (6¹⁄₄ × 12¹⁄₄ in) rectangle, waist band and apron ties from the plain fabric.

Turn under 5 mm (¹⁄₄ in) along one long edge of a rectangle and stitch, placing the raw edge of the lace to the underside of the hem as you sew.

Hem the side edges by turning them under with stitching.

I have used three rows of tucks along the bottom edge of the apron, but they can be used anywhere on a dress or underwear. The width I have used is 5 mm (¹⁄₄ in), with the same distance between the tucks. You can choose any width you desire (if you use tucks on a bodice or yoke, prepare them on rectangle of fabric first, and *then* cut out the pattern pieces).

Now gather the waist end of the apron to fit the waist band by sewing two parallel lines of long stitches between dots indicated on the pattern. Leave loose ends of thread at each end to hold, while pulling the fabric along the two threads and spreading the gathers evenly.

The procedure for attaching the waist band is similar to applying bias tape: fold the band in half lengthwise and press. Lay the gathered end of the apron over one edge of the band and pin, leaving 5 mm (¹⁄₄ in) free on each side. Stitch in place, remove pins and then pull out the lower visible gathering thread. Fold the band over, turning under the seam allowance on it, and slipstitch it to underside (leave side ends open for insertion of ties later).

To make the ties, hem the long sides on each piece first. Fold each end in half lengthwise and stitch with a diagonal stitch. Trim the seam allowance, turn right-side out and press. Stitch to hold forming a triangle at each end.

Insert the other ends (straight) into the side openings on the waist band and stitch over.

Cap

Cut two cap circles (page 36) out of fabric. Stitch the circles together along outer edges, leaving a gap through which to turn right-side out. Trim seam allowance, turn right-side out and press. Slipstitch the opening closed. Stitch a strip of elastic around inside the cap, 3 cm (1¹⁄₈ in) away from the edge, making an instant frill.

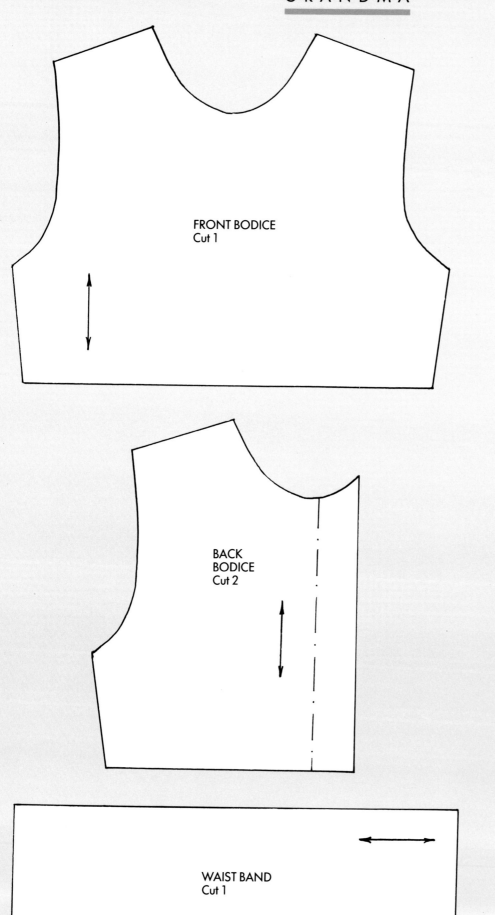

FRONT BODICE
Cut 1

BACK
BODICE
Cut 2

TIES
Cut 2

WAIST BAND
Cut 1

GRANDPA

MATERIALS

Beard 25 g (1 oz) thin yarn
Glasses 30 cm (11¾ in) picture wire
Shirt 15 × 65 cm (6 × 25⅝ in) plain light-weight fabric and 8 cm (3¼ in) sew-on fastening tape (5 mm (¼ in) width)
Trousers 23 × 44 cm (9 × 17⅜ in) plain medium-weight fabric and two small buttons
Waistcoat 14 × 52 cm (5½ × 20½ in) plain medium-weight fabric
Cap 15 × 31 cm (6 × 12¼ in) plain medium-weight fabric

INSTRUCTIONS

Doll's body

Make the Basic Doll with ears (page 12), closing the top of the head, and with no socks.

Using the pattern on page 61 wind a yarn around it to make a beard. Cut the wrapped yarn off the card with a single straight cut, lay it out flat, and then stitch through the middle.

Take the end strands to each side behind the ear, bringing them together at the back of the head and stitch in place. Fold the beard in half at the seam line, then hand stitch it around the face just under the chin.

Unravel individual strands of yarn with a fine-tooth comb for fullness and trim the beard to required length.

Glasses

Take the piece of picture wire and wind it around a pen or pencil once 10 cm (4 in) from one end, forming a circle. Leave a small gap and make another circle in the same way. Adjust the length of the ends, and hand stitch the glasses at the sides of the head.

Shirt

Using the patterns on pages 33–4, cut one back bodice, two front bodices, sleeves, cuffs and collar pieces out of plain fabric.

Sew the shoulder seams of the front bodice sections to the back bodice and turn under the front opening with stitching to form facings.

Slash and hem the sleeve openings and make pleats at the wrist ends as indicated on the pattern. To make cuffs, stitch the four pieces together into two pairs around the curved edges, carefully trim the seam allowance to 2 mm (⅛ in), turn right-side out and press.

To set the sleeves into the armholes, sew two lines of gathering stitches around sleeve heads 1 cm (⅜ in) apart, between dots indicated on the pattern, and pull the gathers to ease the sleeve crowns. Lay the garment out flat and match the side edge of the bodice with the sleeve underarm edge. Pin the sleeve heads to the armholes. Stitch, remove the pins, and pull out visible gathering thread.

Sew the underarm seam and the side seam of bodice in one operation.

Attach the cuffs to the wrist end of the sleeves from one slash to the other. Sew a 5 mm (¼ in) piece of fastening tape to each cuff for easy dressing and removal.

Make a shirt collar by stitching the two pieces together around the outer edges, trim the seam allowance to 2 mm ($^1/_8$ in), turn right-side out and press. Stitch one side of the collar's neck edge to the outside neck edge of the shirt. Slipstitch the other side of the collar to the inside of the neckline. Top-stitch along the dotted line on the collar to form a foldline.

Hem the shirt by turning it under with stitching.

Sew the remaining piece of fastening tape along the facings on the front of the shirt. (I sewed the tape on here with a zigzag stitch, giving the shirt a decorative look.)

Trousers

Cut two trouser pieces (page 57) and two shoulder straps (page 98) out of fabric.

Hem the top and bottom of each trouser piece, sew along both crotch seams and then inner leg seam.

To make shoulder straps, fold each strip of fabric in half lengthwise and stitch along the length, closing one end of each. Trim the seam allowance to 2 mm ($^1/_8$ in), turn right-side out and press. Topstitch close to both edges if desired.

Stitch finished shoulder straps to inside of back waist, cross them over the shoulders and stitch them to the outside of the front. Sew on the buttons.

Cap

Using the patterns on pages 44 and 36, cut two cap circles (one of them with a hole in the centre), one band and two brim pieces out of fabric.

Stitch the cap circles around the outer edges, carefully trim the seam allowance to 2 mm ($^1/_8$ in), turn the right-side out and press.

Fold the band in half lengthwise, stitch the side seam closed and start pinning the inner edge of the cap circle along the band. When you have eased in the curve so that it fits with no unwanted pleats appearing, stitch and remove pins.

Make a brim by stitching the two pieces together along their outer edges, trim the seam allowance carefully to 2 mm ($^1/_8$ in), turn right-side out and press.

Stitch the brim into the band (with side seam of the band lying opposite the centre of the brim).

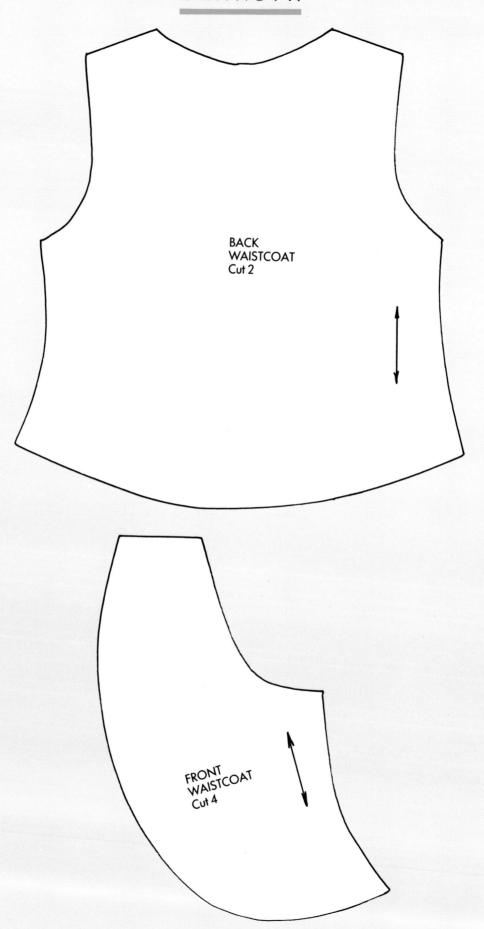

BACK
WAISTCOAT
Cut 2

FRONT
WAISTCOAT
Cut 4

ℛED ℛIDING ℋOOD

MATERIALS

Shoelaces 61 cm (24 in) strand of strong yarn or thread

Underpants 9 × 30 cm (3½ × 11¾ in) plain light-weight fabric and 30 cm (11¾ in) narrow lace edging

Shirt 13 × 78 cm (5⅛ × 30¾ in) plain light-weight fabric; 20 cm (8 in) narrow elastic and 1 cm (⅜ in) sew-on fastening tape

Skirt 14 × 61 cm (5½ × 24 in) checked light-weight fabric; 61 cm (24 in) narrow lace edging and 1 cm (⅜ in) sew-on fastening tape

Cloak 30 × 50 cm (11¾ × 19¾ in) medium-weight fabric; 30 × 50 cm (11¾ × 19¾ in) lining and 50 cm (19¾ in) narrow ribbon

INSTRUCTIONS

Doll's body

Make the Basic Doll (page 12) with long hair and knee-socks.

To make plaits, stitch the hair along the back and sides of the head just above the neckline and divide the hair in two equal parts at the nape. Plait the strands of each side and tie off the ends with the same thread or yarn as used for the hair. Trim ends to even lengths on each plait.

Make two ribbon bows by cutting the piece of ribbon in half and crossing the ends. Stitch around the middle with a thread of the same colour. Apply a thin layer of glue to the ends and trim them when they are dry.

Stitch a bow to the end of each plait.

Embroider a few cross-stitches with a single strand of yarn or strong thread on the front of the shoes for laces.

Underpants

Using the pattern on page 40, cut two underpants pieces out of fabric.

Turn under 5 mm (¼ in) along the lower edges on each piece, place strips of lace edging on the underside of the hem so that the scalloped edge falls just below hemline and stitch.

Hem the waist edge and join pieces to each other by stitching along both crotch seams and then inner leg seams.

Shirt

Using the patterns on pages 42, 22 and 24, cut one front, two back bodices, sleeves and collar pieces out of fabric.

Sew the shoulder seams of the front bodice to the back bodice sections.

Make short full sleeves with frills by turning up a 2 cm (¾ in) deep hem at the sleeve ends and stitching a 10 cm (4 in) piece of elastic along with the hem. Stretch the elastic to fit as you sew.

Sew two lines of gathering stitches around the sleeve heads 1 cm (⅜ in) apart and between dots indicated on the pattern. Pull the gathers evenly to fit the armholes. Lay out the garment flat and match side edge of bodice with sleeve underarm edge. Pin the sleeve heads to the armholes. To join sleeves to the rest of the shirt, stitch the seam through the middle of the two gathered rows, remove the pins and then pull out the lower visible gathering thread.

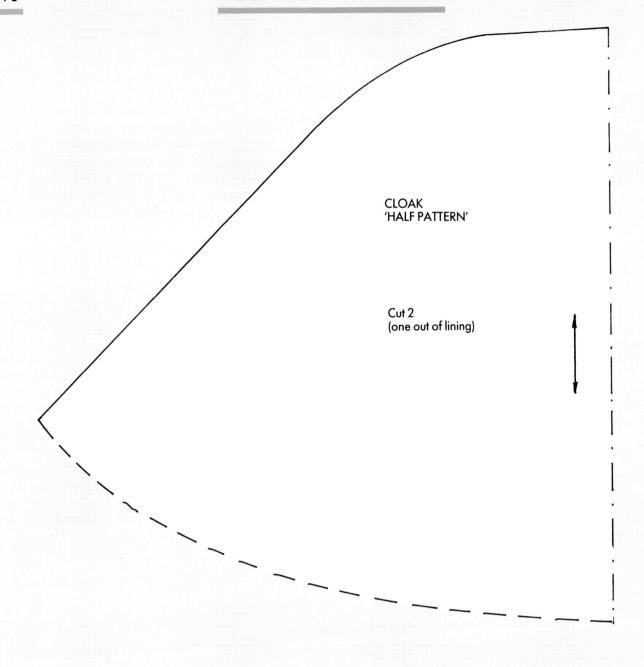

CLOAK
'HALF PATTERN'

Cut 2
(one out of lining)

WAIST BAND 'HALF PATTERN'
Cut 1

$\mathcal{S}$ANTA $\mathcal{C}$LAUS

MATERIALS

Moustache and beard 25 g (1 oz) thin white yarn
Coat, trousers and cap 21 × 134 cm (8$\frac{1}{4}$ × 52$\frac{3}{4}$ in) red medium-weight fabric; 7 × 118 cm (2$\frac{3}{4}$ × 46$\frac{1}{2}$ in) white fleece, 25 cm (9$\frac{7}{8}$ in) narrow red bias binding tape, 20 cm (8 in) narrow elastic and oddment of yarn for pom-pom
Sash 50 cm (19$\frac{3}{4}$ in) black cord
Boots 11 × 40 cm (4$\frac{3}{8}$ × 15$\frac{3}{4}$ in) black or brown felt
Gloves 5 × 20 cm (2 × 8 in) red felt
Sack 20 × 25 cm (8 × 10 in) brown felt
Extra stuffing for belly and sack

INSTRUCTIONS

Doll's body

Make the Basic Doll with ears (page 12), closing the top of the head and with no socks.

Using the pattern on page 61, wind a yarn around it to make beard. Cut the wrapped yarn off the card with a single straight cut, lay it out flat, and then stitch through the middle.

Take the end strands to each side behind the ear, bringing them together at the back of the head and stitch in place. Fold the beard in half at the seam line then hand-stitch it around the face just under the chin.

Unravel individual strands of yarn with a fine-tooth comb for fullness and trim the beard to the required length.

Embroider the moustache with the same thread or yarn as used for the beard.

Coat

Cut a pair of front bodices, one back bodice and sleeves from red fabric plus a 65 × 7 cm (25$\frac{5}{8}$ × 2$\frac{3}{4}$ in) strip from white fleece for the trim, the hat band and sleeve bands.

Join the front bodice sections to the back at the shoulders.

Fold the sleeve bands in half lengthwise and pin them to the bottom edge of the sleeves. Stitch and remove the pins.

Now lay out the garment flat and match the side edge of the bodice with the sleeve underarm edge. Pin the sleeve heads to the armholes. Stitch and remove the pins.

Sew the underarm seam and the side seam of bodice in one operation.

Now fold the trim for the coat in half, and starting at the top of the front opening, stitch the band down one side, along the entire bottom, ending at the top of the other side.

To bind the neck edge, unfold one raw edge of the binding tape, place it to the right side of the coat (with bias tape edge level with the neck edge of the coat), and stitch along the crease of the binding. Fold the other pressed edge of bias tape to the wrong side of the coat, turn in the ends on each side and slip-stitch along the hem.

Tie a knot in from each end of the sash, unravelling the ends for fullness.

Put the coat on the doll and make a pad of stuffing to form a belly. Hand stitch the coat closed, overlapping the white trim.

Trousers

Cut two trouser pieces (page 57) out of fabric.

Turn under 5 mm ($^1/_4$ in) along lower and upper edges on both pieces.

Join two pieces to each other by stitching along one crotch seam only. Open out the joined piece so it is flat and make a casing at the waist. Thread a 20 cm (8 in) piece of narrow elastic through with a safety pin. Stretch the elastic to fit the doll's waist and secure.

Fold the trousers in half, and stitch the other crotch seam closed. Stitch over twice at casing to reinforce the seam.

Re-fold trousers into their finished form and stitch inner leg seam closed.

Cap

Cut a cap piece from red fabric and a band from white fleece.

Stitch the band to the bottom of the cap. Join the side seam, trim the seam allowance and turn right-side out.

To make a pom-pom, wind the strand of yarn around three of your fingers and slip it off. Stitch around the middle with a strong thread or yarn of same colour. Cut the sides loose, trim and ruffle to make a ball. Hand stitch the pom-pom at the point of the cap.

Boots

Cut two boot pieces from felt.

Fold each piece in half and stitch all sides except the top. Trim the seam allowance and turn right-side out. Fold the boot top over to form a trim.

Sack

Fold the rectangle of fabric in half width-wise and stitch three sides closed leaving a short one open. Turn right-side out and stuff loosely.

Use a piece of cord or crochet thread to tie the bag closed.

Gloves

Cut four glove pieces.

Stitch in pairs along the curved edges, trim the seam allowance and turn right-side out.

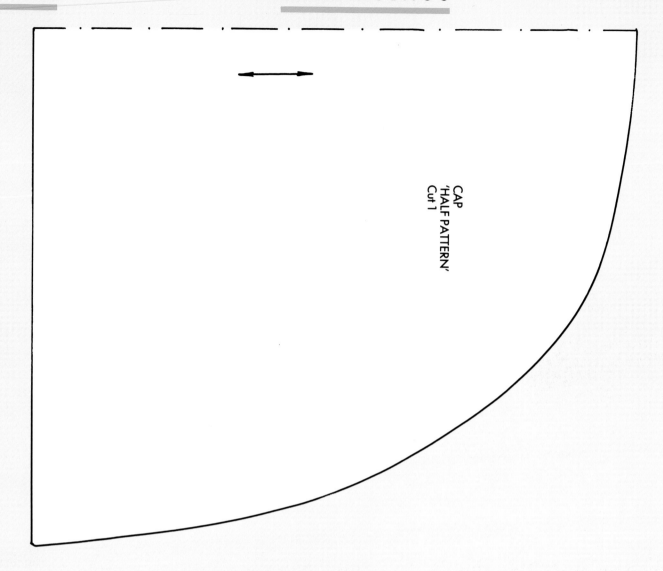

CAP
'HALF PATTERN'
Cut 1

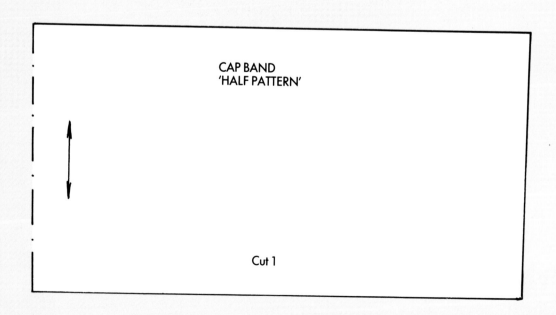

CAP BAND
'HALF PATTERN'

Cut 1

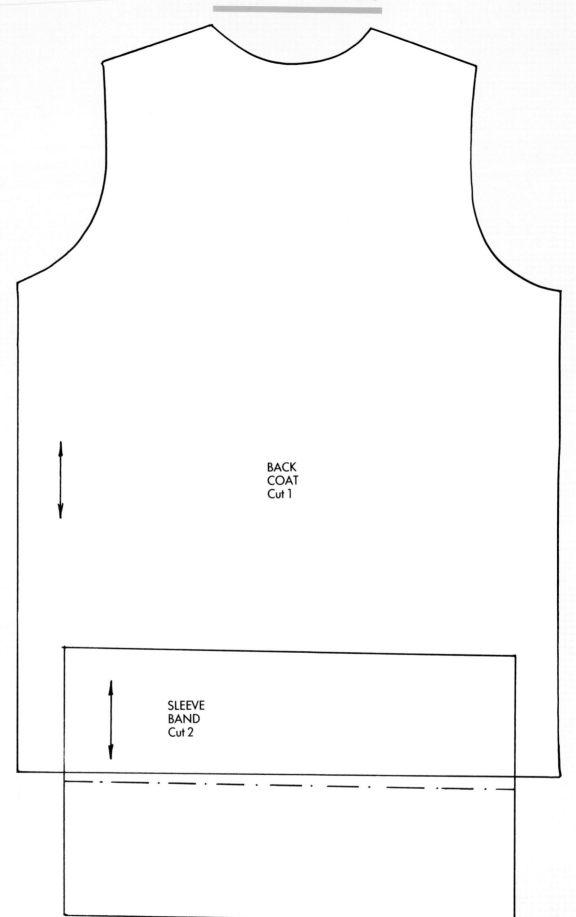

BACK
COAT
Cut 1

SLEEVE
BAND
Cut 2

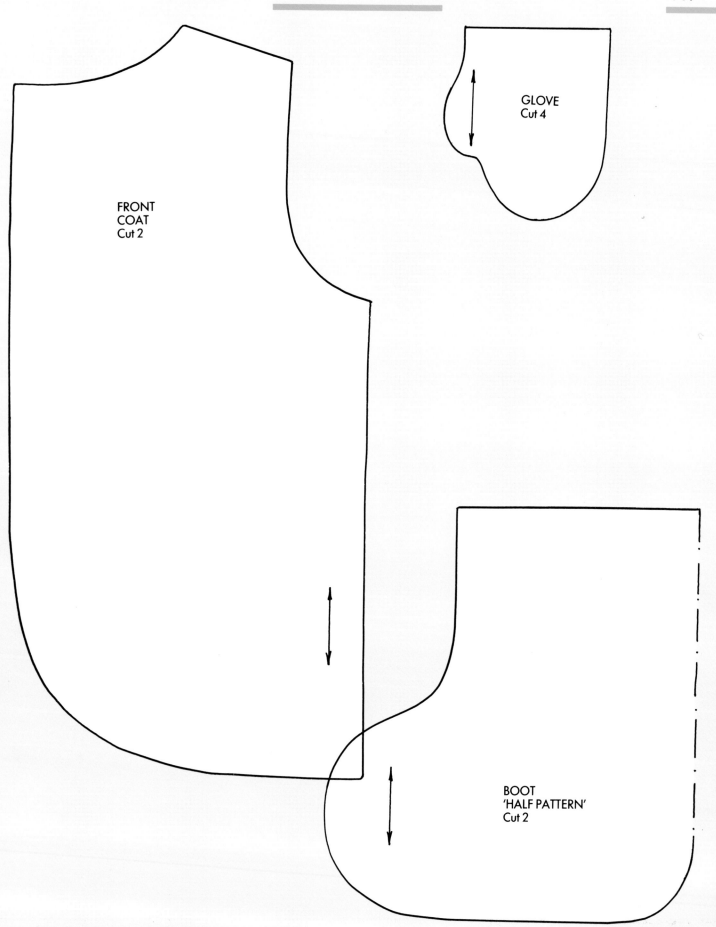

GLOVE
Cut 4

FRONT
COAT
Cut 2

BOOT
'HALF PATTERN'
Cut 2

ＳLEEPY ＧIRL

MATERIALS

Underpants 9 × 30 cm (3½ × 11¾ in) plain light-weight fabric and 30 cm (11¾ in) narrow lace edging
Nightdress 23 × 92 cm (9 × 36¼ in) spotted light-weight fabric; 20 cm (8 in) narrow elastic; 16 cm (6⅜ in) narrow bias binding tape and four small buttons
Nightcap 20 × 24 cm (8 × 9½ in) plain light-weight fabric and oddment of yarn for tassel
Bear 15 × 24 cm (6 × 9½ in) brown fleece; 10 cm (4 in) narrow ribbon; extra stuffing and 50 cm (19¾ in) strong black thread

INSTRUCTIONS

Doll's body

Make the Basic Doll (page 12) with long hair and ankle-socks.

To make plaits, stitch the hair along the back and sides of the head just above the neckline and divide the hair in two equal parts at the nape. Plait the strands of each side and tie off the ends with the same thread or yarn as used for the hair. Trim the ends to even lengths on each plait.

Underpants

Using the pattern on page 40, cut two underpants pieces out of fabric.

Turn under 5 mm (¼ in) along the lower edges on each piece, place strips of lace edging on the underside of the hem so that the scalloped edge falls just below hemline and stitch.

Hem the waist edges and join pieces to each other by stitching along both crotch seams and inner leg seams.

Nightdress

Cut a pair of front skirt panels, one back panel, the front and back yokes, and the sleeves from the fabric.

To gather the skirt, sew two parallel lines of long stitches 1 cm (⅜ in) apart between the dots indicated on the top edges of the skirt panels. Leave the loose ends of the thread at each end to hold, while pulling the fabric along the two threads, and spreading the gathers evenly.

Now pin the gathered top edges of the front skirt panel to the front yokes, and back skirt panel to back yoke. Stitch the seam through the middle of the two gathered rows, remove pins and then pull out the lower visible gathering thread.

Join the front yokes to the back at the shoulders.

Make long full sleeves with frills by hemming the sleeve ends and stitching a 10 cm (4 in) piece of elastic 2 cm (¾ in) from the hemmed edge. Stretch the elastic to fit as you sew.

Sew two lines of gathering stitches around the sleeve heads and pull the gathers evenly to fit the armholes. Lay out the garment flat and match side edge of bodice with sleeve underarm edge. Pin the sleeve heads to the armholes. To join sleeves to the rest of the dress, stitch the seam through the middle of the two gathered rows, remove the pins and then pull out the lower visible gathering thread.

Sew underarm seam and side seam of dress in one operation.

Turn under front opening and press to form facings. Make buttonholes along left side of the facing. Sew buttons to the right side.

Hem the bottom of the dress by turning it under with stitching but pay attention to curved edges.

To bind the neck edge, unfold one raw edge of the binding tape, place it to the right side of the dress (with bias tape edge level with the neck edge), and stitch along the crease of the binding. Fold the other pressed edge of bias tape to the wrong side of the dress, turn in the ends on each side and slipstitch along the hem.

Bear

First trace the Bear pattern on two layers of fleece, and before cutting it out, sew with a small stitch all around, following the traced marks. Leave a gap at one side for turning right-side out. Trim the seam allowance, turn right-side out, stuff loosely leaving the ears empty. Slipstitch the opening closed. Stitch over the base of both ears to differentiate them, and embroider eyes and nose.

Make a ribbon bow by crossing the ends and stitching around the middle with a thread of the same colour. Apply a thin layer of glue to the ends and trim them when dry. Stitch the bow to the bear.

Nightcap

Cut a cap piece from fabric.

Turn under the bottom edge with stitching. Join the side seam, trim the seam allowance and turn right-side out.

Make a tassel by winding a strand of yarn around the tassel card. Cut the wrapped yarn off the card with a single straight cut and knot a strand of yarn round centre. Now fold at centre and tie the same strand of yarn round (as for a knot), about 1 cm (^{3}/$_8$ in) from the top, bringing it through the top again. Trim the end to even length.

Attach the tassel to the top of the nightcap, starting the yarn from the inside of the cap.

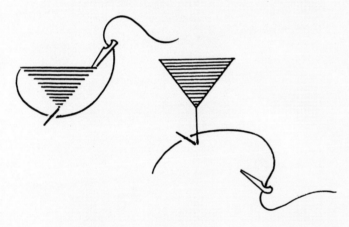

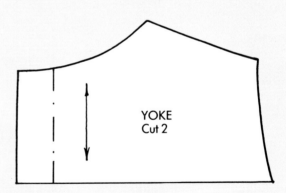

YOKE
Cut 2

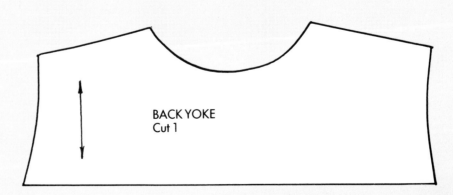

BACK YOKE
Cut 1

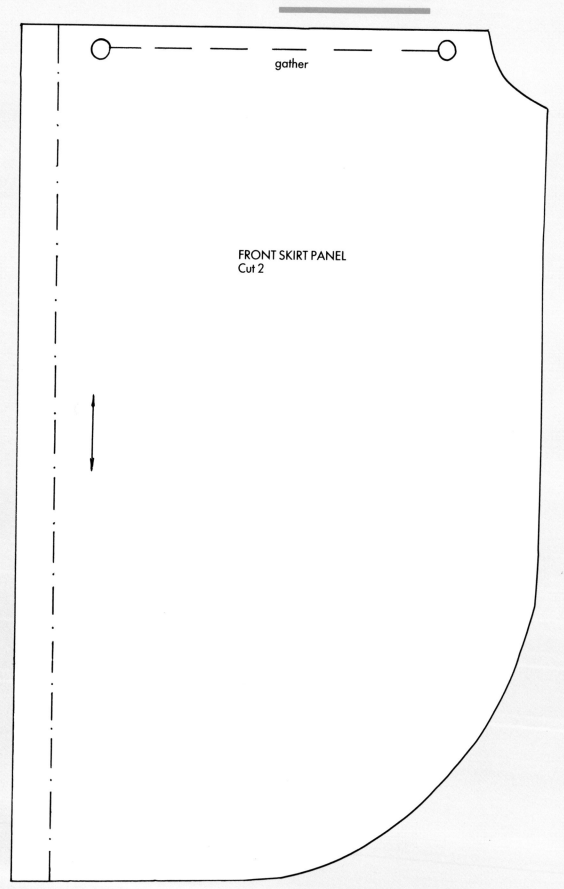

gather

FRONT SKIRT PANEL
Cut 2

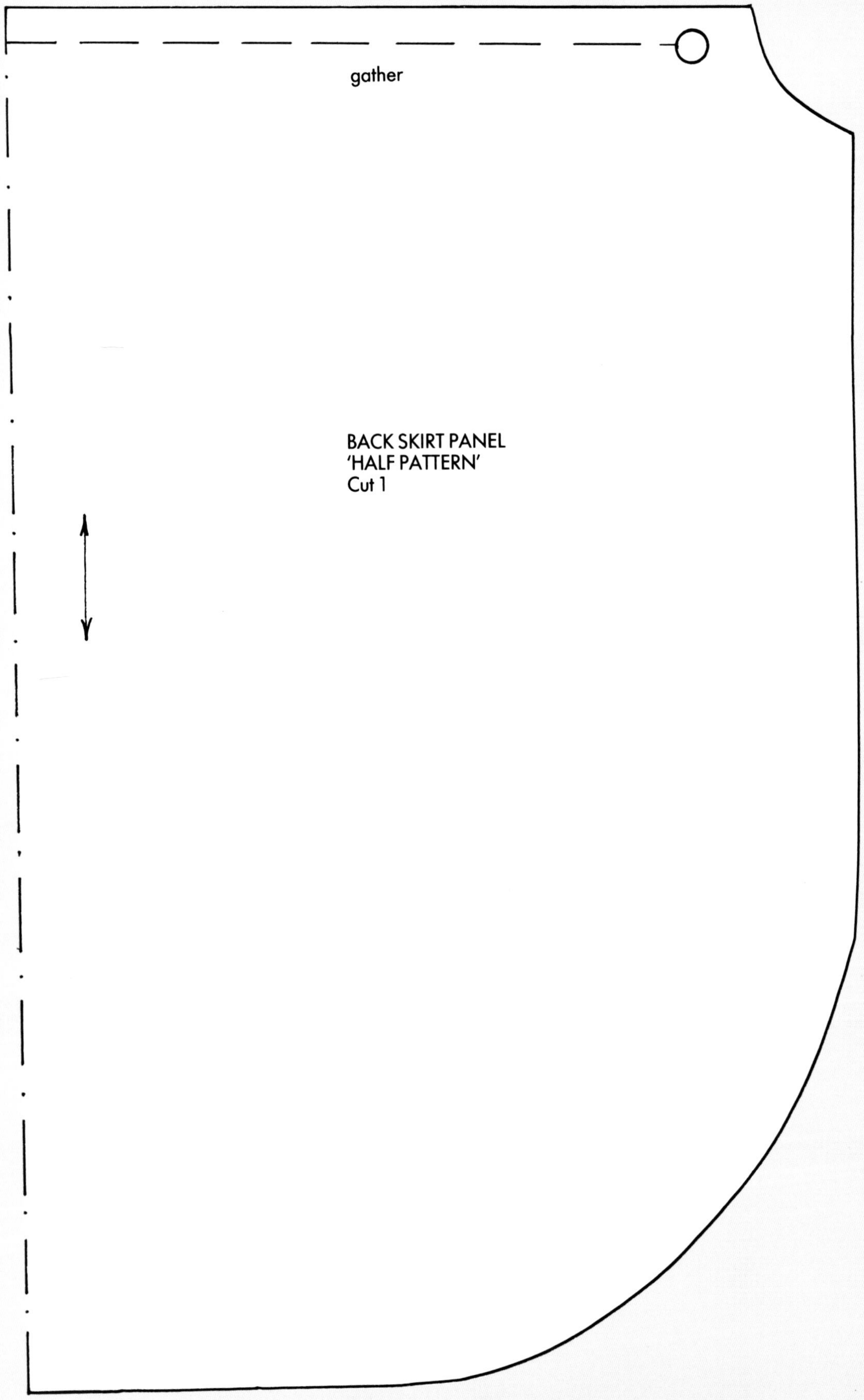

gather

BACK SKIRT PANEL
'HALF PATTERN'
Cut 1

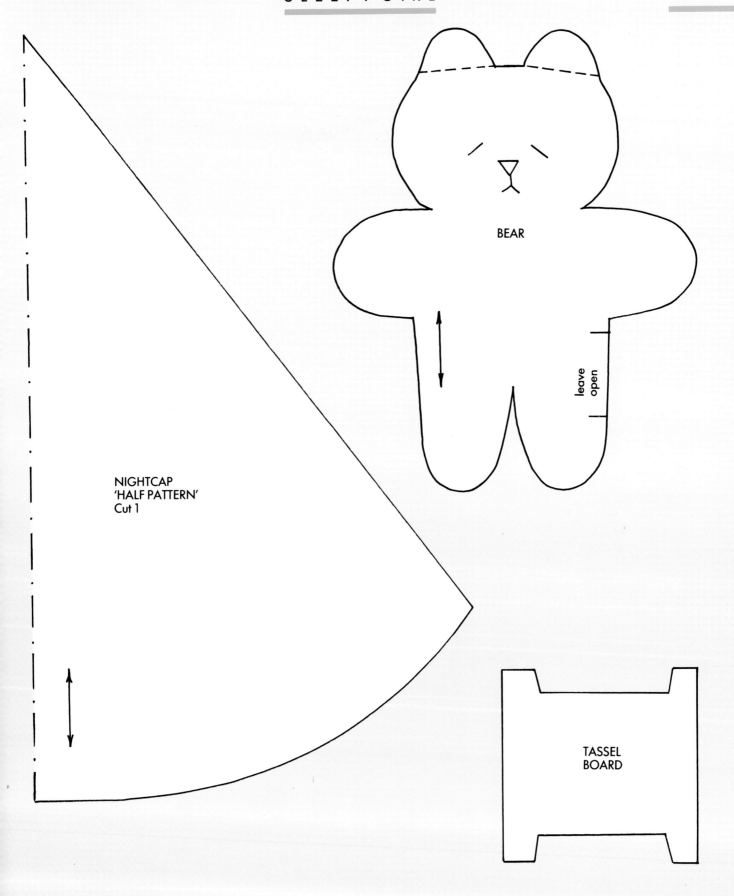

NIGHTCAP
'HALF PATTERN'
Cut 1

BEAR

leave open

TASSEL
BOARD

$\mathcal{G}$IFT $\mathcal{B}$OX

This box is very useful if you want to give your doll as a present, or even make one to sell. The box is very simple to make, and also inexpensive.

MATERIALS

37 × 44 cm (14⁵/₈ × 17³/₈ in) coverboard
15.5 × 30 cm (6¹/₈ × 11³/₄ in) clear acetate
Craft knife or scissors
Pencil
Ruler
Pair of compasses
Glue
Cutting mat or board

INSTRUCTIONS

First of all, draw the box on the back of the coverboard using the measurements given. To draw the curved edges, use a pair of compasses or even a plate or saucepan lid for guidance.

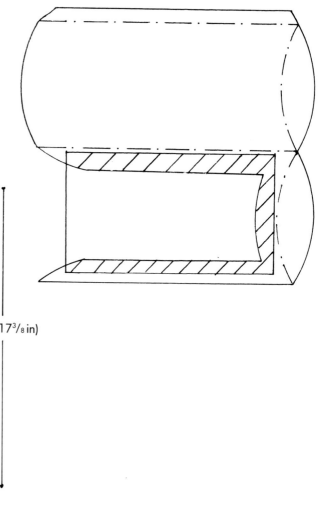

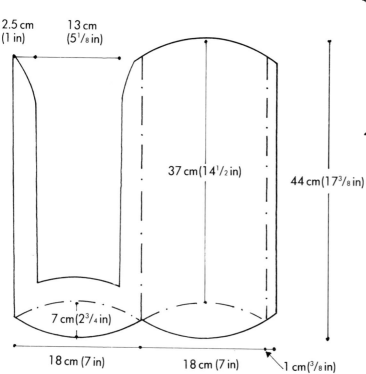

2.5 cm (1 in) 13 cm (5¹/₈ in)

37 cm (14¹/₂ in)

44 cm (17³/₈ in)

7 cm (2³/₄ in)

18 cm (7 in)   18 cm (7 in)   1 cm (³/₈ in)

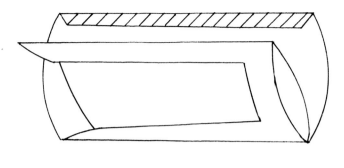

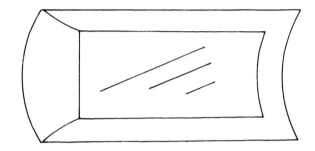

Now score along the fold-lines with the blunt point of a pair of scissors, taking care not to tear the card.

Cut with a craft knife or scissors.

Now apply glue to the shaded area of the box illustrated and press acetate onto it.

When the glue dries, apply another layer to the edge of the box, and join to the front.

When the glue dries, fold in the bottom of the box along the scored curves.